Looking Good

SMART TALK

Looking Good

Susan Sloate

Troll Associates

Library of Congress Cataloging-in-Publication Data

Sloate, Susan.
　　Looking good / by Susan Sloate; Donald Richey, illustrator.
　　　p.　　cm.—(Smart talk)
　　Summary: Discusses how to feature and improve upon your natural physical attributes by selecting, coordinating, or creating clothing and fashion accessories.
　　ISBN 0-8167-1999-3 (lib. bdg.)　ISBN 0-8167-2000-2 (pbk.)
　　1. Clothing and dress—Juvenile literature.　2. Beauty, Personal—Juvenile literature.　[1. Clothing and dress.　2. Beauty, Personal.]　I. Richey, Donald, ill.　II. Title.　III. Series.
TT507.S684　1991
646'.36—dc20　　　　　　　　　　　　　89-28019

Copyright © 1991 by Troll Associates, Mahwah, New Jersey
All rights reserved. No part of this book may be used or reproduced in any manner whatsoever without written permission from the publisher.

Printed in the United States of America.
10　9　8　7　6　5　4　3　2　1

Table of Contents

Chapter 1 1
Style—What's Yours?

Chapter 2 15
Color—It's Not All Black and
White Anymore!

Chapter 3 21
"The Look"—Which Is Best for You?

Chapter 4 31
Something Extra!

Chapter 5 47
Free and Easy Mood Dressing

Chapter 6 61
Show Off "The Best You!"

Chapter 7 75
When the Going Gets Tough . . .
the Tough Go Shopping!

Chapter 8 89
Recycling

Chapter 9 97
Fashion Smarts

Chapter 10 107
Making It All Work

Style—What's Yours?

*H*ey, you! Yes, you—looking in that mirror. Who do you think you are?

In these years, finding out *who you are* is the greatest preoccupation of most girls. What do I want? What do I think? What do I look like? It's a time for exploration into the greatest mystery of all—*you*.

One key to who you are—and how you express yourself to others—is in the way you dress. Your clothes indicate your style, your personality, your own uniqueness. The right clothes for you can accent your best self.

Choosing a wardrobe that fits your particular style and personality can be both a challenge and a pleasure. That means discovering which colors, fabrics and fashion looks suit you best and bring out the best in you. Remember, "what looks best" is likely to change as you get older, but nothing should prevent you from experimenting *now*. Fashion can always be fun!

Meet three typical girls. Like you, they go to school, go out on the weekends and are involved in a-thousand-and-one exciting activities. And like you, they have typical fashion questions:

MARCY—She's tall, blonde and lean, an athlete by inclination and build. Her favorite activities involve strenuous exercise, and she loves to feel comfortable and relaxed in her clothes. How can she best show off those long legs and lanky frame?

LINDA—She's petite and dark-haired, a bookworm by nature, and developing a curvy figure. She'd rather spend an afternoon curled up with a book than participating in any kind of outdoor activity. She wants to find her best fashion colors and fabrics so she can show off her shiny hair and petite size to their best advantage!

KIM—A fiery redhead with fair skin and freckles, who adores the latest music, the latest movies, the latest fashions. She knows what's in style and she loves to be involved in it—how can she develop a dynamite look?

Let Marcy, Linda and Kim guide you through the fashion maze, as they learn what looks great on them—and help *you* learn what looks great on *you*!

YOUR BODY TYPE

Where do you start? With your body. What's your body type? To figure out your type, you must consider three elements: height, weight and bone structure.

HEIGHT

Are you tall? Petite? Medium-sized? Height plays a major role in determining body type. While you have not yet grown to your full height, you probably have a pretty good idea of just how tall you will grow. If by age twelve you're over five feet tall with a long-lined body, you're likely to be a model's height (5'7" or over) when you stop growing.

If, on the other hand, you're a few inches shy of five feet on your twelfth birthday, you may not grow taller than five feet four inches.

If you're in the five-foot range right now, but your body is more compact than long-lined, you can expect an adult height in the medium range—five feet four to five feet six inches.

WEIGHT

Weight varies greatly among pre-teen and teenage girls. You might be very slender now, but you're likely to fill out during puberty. Or you could still be shedding baby fat at the age of twelve and turn out to be a streamlined beauty. Important areas to look at include your waist, hips, stomach and bust. Even at your age, these should provide a clue about your eventual weight distribution. For instance, do you have a very slender waist with wide hips? Or no waist or hips to speak of but some extra roundness in your stomach? Is your bust nonexistent or well-developed by age twelve? To find out your weight tendencies, examine these areas carefully in a full-length mirror.

If you've always been able to eat all you want while maintaining your figure—congratulations! You're unlikely to encounter weight problems later on. You'll be one of the last girls to develop a pronounced bust, but you won't have to worry so much about reaching for that second chocolate bar.

Or perhaps you're already trying to curb what you eat. That's because you were among the *first* to develop a bust—but your hips and waist are a little chunkier than you'd like. No problem. It means you'll be growing up with a curvy figure. You're likely to be smaller or medium-sized, while your slender friends are already a head taller and growing toward the sky! It's nothing to worry about. While your tall friends wear simpler styles, you'll be going all out with frills and flowing skirts!

BONE STRUCTURE

Your overall bone structure is the final clue to your body type. Think about both your height and weight—and you'll come up with the answer to what bone structure you have! If you have little or no bust to speak of yet (cup size AA or A) and slim hips and waist, you're likely to be a naturally slender type. These are the girls with "boyish" figures and long slender bones—tiny waists, slender hips, long lovely legs. Naturally slender types will usually develop an adequate—but not overly large—bust, and their bones will sometimes be angular and prominent. They're inclined to be long-waisted—that is, their torsos stretch longer than other girls'. Naturally slender girls can wear dramatic styles and always look great.

If your bust develops to a greater degree (B or C cup) in the next couple of years and you have a slim waistline with pronounced hips, you will tend toward the voluptuous type. Voluptuous girls, when fully-developed, usually have feminine, curvy figures that look terrific in super-feminine styles. Their bones are shorter but slightly larger than the naturally slender types. Their bodies tend to be short-waisted—that is, their torsos are smaller from shoulders to hips than the average girl's.

The voluptuous types are also the girls who tend to put on weight easily—but when their weight is under control, they'll have healthy, attractive figures to be proud of! If you have noticed that your hips tend to be a bit chunky or your bust is larger than average, you can pretty much count yourself a voluptuous type. Be grateful! When those curves are under control, fashion is a bonanza!

The third type is the tomboy. Neither as slim as the naturally slender girl nor as curvy as the voluptuous type, the tomboy will have a slim, compact body with pretty legs—legs that aren't as long as the naturally slender type, but attractive nonetheless. The tomboy's bones are longer than the voluptuous girls' but shorter than the naturally slenders'—and her torso from shoulder to waist is average-sized. The tomboy will seldom develop beyond a B-size bra cup, but her body will always look sturdy and appealing. They are unlikely to grow beyond five feet six, and they'll carry more weight than the naturally slender girl—but their figures aren't made for the cuts and curves of the voluptuous styles.

Marcy, our tall blonde, knows instinctively that she's naturally slender. Already stretching toward the sky, Marcy has an underdeveloped bust but long arms and legs—and she can eat as much as she wants!

Linda, our petite brunette, is a voluptuous type. She will probably not grow taller than five feet four—but she was the first in her class to wear a bra!

Kim, our fiery redhead, is the tomboy type. She's neither long-waisted nor short-waisted, with slim, not-too-long legs and a compact body. As a tomboy, she'll be able to wear a variety of styles with terrific flair!

YOUR PERSONALITY

How you *look* isn't the only factor in deciding who you are. What about your interests—your activities—and your secret goals and dreams? They play a major role in determining your type. Think about who you are and what you want.

INTERESTS

Do you scribble poetry during math class? Or pore over maps of exotic islands? Is your idea of heaven taking apart a car's engine—or taking a ride in a private plane? Or are you just caught up in shopping with friends?

Your interests, oddly enough, often match your body type. If you're tall and slim and well-coordinated, you may be a sports nut—playing tennis, golf, racquetball or volleyball in school—and organizing your own games on weekends! Petite girls often prefer horseback riding or exploring in caves—where they can squeeze into tiny places no one else can! Medium-sized girls may lean toward climbing or acrobatics.

Don't feel limited by your shape, however. Any interest can be pursued by girls of every body type. Do you paint whenever you're home? Or shoot hoops? Or write songs? Are you crazy about historical fiction—or do you prefer memorizing your favorite rock band's last thirty songs?

ACTIVITIES

What do you do when you have spare time? Do you spend it alone, join a school club, try out for team sports, or just hang out with friends?

Girls with a strong sense of self can enjoy their leisure time alone. They're usually so interested in the short story they're working on or the video project they've started for class that they don't even notice the lack of company! They can be creative—whether it's writing a song or devising a new type of engine—or explorative—staying after school to work on advanced algebra problems or prowling the libraries for more information on a never-solved mystery! In any case, you'll always find them doing something interesting and absorbing.

Athletes have their own special style. Whether alone or on a team, they concentrate their enormous energies on their sport. They may be in the center of a crowd of cheering fans—but their mind is on the game!

The social girls spend lots of time with their friends. Nothing is more fun for them than prowling the local mall with their closest girlfriends! Or organizing parties and sleep-overs so they can be together even more!

The social girls are always at the center of a crowd—and they love every second of it!

GOALS AND DREAMS

Loners and athletes have dreams they can almost touch. These goals are so important to them that sometimes the world they're living in seems dim and unreal by comparison. The loner might want to paint the world's best portrait or write the great American novel. She might want to hunt down a criminal who was never found—or be part of a team to raise the *Titanic*—or explore the North Pole!

The athlete's mind is on becoming faster—stronger—better able to endure—and she has to do it *now*! She is just as ambitious as the loner, but her ambitions center on the game. Winning—or setting a record—are the goals most important to her.

The social butterfly lives for today, as well—but her goals are much less defined. Being with her friends, giving a great party and getting into the club she wants are her ambitions. What comes tomorrow is not her concern. She's a bubbling, sparkling, terrific companion—and she'll be that way at parties, on dates and at every kind of social event!

★★★

Let's see how our young fashion guides measure their own personalities:

Marcy is the athlete of the group. She'll play any game, but especially favors tennis, swimming and basketball, and her ambitions lie in one day becoming a professional. She's serious about her sports dreams and works hard to fulfill them.

Linda is a loner, who dreams of faraway places and great adventures! She's perfectly happy studying a travel guide, watching documentaries about explorers or checking out the library for the latest news about underwater adventure! Some day she wants to be part of it all—but for now she's happy to participate from afar, curled up in her favorite chair at home.

Kim is the social butterfly of the crowd. She's always surrounded by a group of girls chattering excitedly, and she's the first to propose a party or a trip to the mall. Contemporary and interested in everything around her, Kim enjoys living for today.

THE WELL-DRESSED CLOSET

Open the door of your closet and take a good, hard look inside. What does your wardrobe look like?

Do you have twenty terrific "dressy" outfits—but only two skirts for school? Or a year's worth of wonderful mix 'n' match school clothes—without a single item suitable for a tough after-school workout? Have you ever looked at your wardrobe and wailed, "I haven't got a thing to wear"?

Everybody has. The reason is usually *not* a lack of clothing, but a lack of understanding how to plan your wardrobe. Taking a few minutes to figure out what you *really* need can save you hours of anguish in the long run.

The solution to structuring your wardrobe lies in *how much time* you spend at various activities. You'll want to have the greatest variety in the type of clothes you wear most often.

A Sample School Wardrobe

Where do you spend the majority of your time? In school, right? Five days a week, for six hours or more a day, you need clothes that will look and feel right for classes and after-school clubs. This means your basic school wardrobe should include:

- *two skirts*
- *four blouses*
- *two dresses*
- *four sweaters*
- *three pairs of pants (or jeans) suitable for the classroom*

The next largest clothes category for young women is sports, or comfortable clothes. You don't spend as much time at sports or hanging out on Saturday morning as you do in school, but it's essential, nonetheless, to own some comfortable, stretchy, easy-to-wash clothes for those times when you just want to relax—or play your favorite sport! You'll want to own at least two pairs of jeans, one sweat suit, one or two sweat shirts, and three short-sleeved shirts. If you love a particular sport, you'll need at least one outfit that you wear *exclusively* for that sport—such as a tennis outfit, a leotard and tights for a workout or jodhpurs and boots for horseback riding.

A Sample Sports Wardrobe

- 2 pairs jeans/one designer, one not
- One gray sweat suit with dark red trim
- One long-sleeved white sweat shirt
- 3 short-sleeved shirts: red, blue and green
- 2 leotards/blue and gray
- 1 pair aerobic shoes
- 2 pairs heavy tights
- 1 tennis outfit/white
- 1 pair tennis shoes

Naturally, you need some dressier clothes for dates—clothes that will look great for weekend movie dates, informal dances and parties at friends' houses. These are the clothes that say "Wow!" to everyone who sees you in them. They're eye-catching, sleek and just too dressy for school. You might want to own as many as three combination outfits—jumpsuits, pants and matching shirts, or a knockout dress in some exotic fabric. You can get away with fewer items if you spend less time at social events—or you might want to plan for a couple more if you're the outgoing type who parties every weekend!

A Sample Dress Wardrobe

- 1 cotton jumpsuit
- 1 pair silky pants with matching shirt in a bright shimmery color

- 1 full skirt with peasant blouse
- 1 mini dress

What about those *extra*-special occasions? The knockout New Year's Eve party, the oh-so-formal Christmas dance at the country club, the occasional *super* wedding—they demand something really special! However, these occasions are few and far between, and you will need very few clothes to meet the demand. One special outfit for fall/winter and one for spring/summer should prepare you for any holiday affair. (If you live in a climate of year-round warm weather, such as Florida, Texas or southern California, one outfit will look perfect for every special occasion throughout the year.)

When you take the time to figure out what you really wear and how often, you're taking the first step toward assembling a wardrobe that will suit you on every occasion!

✩✩ LOOKING GOOD QUIZ ✩✩

For all quizzes, please write your answers on a separate sheet of paper.

Answer true or false to the questions below to test your ability to determine your own personal style.

1. *If you're the tomboy type, you're likely to be the first girl at school to develop a bust.*
   True or False
2. *If you're a social butterfly, you can't be a naturally slender type.*
   True or False

3. *Most tomboy types are athletic.*
    True or False
4. *Naturally slender types tend to have the longest legs of any of the three body types.*
    True or False
5. *Voluptuous types have a tendency to gain unwanted weight.*
    True or False
6. *You can be both a tomboy type and a naturally slender type at the same time.*
    True or False
7. *If you love to take apart engines to study, you're likely to be a loner.*
    True or False
8. *Athletes have a contemporary, live-for-today attitude.*
    True or False
9. *Loners are not goal-oriented.*
    True or False
10. *You can be any body type and still be an athlete.*
    True or False

Answers: 1. False 2. False 3. False 4. True 5. True 6. False 7. True 8. True 9. False 10. True

☆☆☆

Color—It's Not All Black and White Anymore!

True or False?
1. Blondes can never wear certain colors.
2. Red on a redhead is a no-no.
3. Brunettes should always avoid black and white.
The answers to all of the above? False!

How much do you know about color? Do you know that certain colors can give you a glow, while other colors don't? Do you know that certain colors pick up your mood—while others might tend to quiet you down? Do you know that no matter *what* your coloring is, you can probably wear almost *any* color you wish?

It's true! Color is one of the fundamentals of smart dressing. Choosing colors that complement your skin, hair and eyes can make all the difference in your overall appearance. Wearing the right shades to set off your natural coloring is an easy and marvelously effective tool in creating your own special look.

After all, the *first* thing people notice about your clothes is their color. Why not use color to give yourself a boost?

COLORS FOR BLONDES—Pastels are Prettiest!

Are you a blonde? "Blond" hair ranges in shade from a wheat color often described as "yellow" or "golden"—to a silver known as "white blond." Blond hair mixed with light brown can be a pale copper color. It's a shade that can look wonderful combined with the right colors!

Skin tones for blondes range from very fair to an occasional olive. It's not uncommon for blondes to sport light freckles across their nose and upper cheeks. Their eyes tend to be blue, green, light brown or gray.

Blondes always look best in soft pastel colors, which accent their light hair, eyes and skin. Their hair shimmers against the glow of a soft violet, light green, powder blue or delicate pink. Fair-haired girls blossom under the influence of light beige or pale yellow.

If you're a blonde who loves red, you can wear it! Just be sure to choose a very soft red, not a fire-engine color. It'll blend with your skin and hair and make you look dazzling! Blondes also look wonderful in ivory (off-white) and especially good in black. An ivory and black outfit really plays up that luminous hair!

Marcy, our long-legged blonde, says purple is her favorite color, but she can't wear purple comfortably in its brightest shades. Instead, she chooses a soft lilac mixed with pink—and gets compliments from all her friends!

MARCY'S BEST COLORS

- Soft pink
- Soft lilac
- Pale yellow
- Light gray
- Black
- Soft red
- Ivory
- Light green
- Powder blue
- Pale beige

BRUNETTE—Brights are Best!

Are you a brunette? "Brunette" hair refers to any shade of color from the softest light brown to the blackest black. Such hair sometimes features reddish highlights, which can be classified as "auburn."

Brunettes vary in skin tone from fair to golden beige, to deep olive to a dark mahogany.

Eye color varies greatly with brunettes. Most sport dark brown, black or hazel eyes. But others feature deep blue, green or gray eyes. No single group embraces a larger eye-color range than brunettes.

Brunettes look best in clear primary and secondary colors that set off their burnished hair. They'll choose bright red, gleaming emerald green, royal blue, icy white, deep purple—and they'll look great! These vivid colors pick up the lights in brunette hair, eyes and skin—and you can throw in a bright yellow or soft silver for variety!

Girls with darker skin can enhance their skin tone by wearing darker shades of their favorite colors. Deep yellows, dark greens, royal purples and midnight blues give them even more sparkle!

Linda, our dazzling brunette, glows in red and wears it in several shades: bright red for her windbreaker, cherry red in her sweater, and a deep burgundy in her favorite dress. She also favors stark white—and black, which sets off her lovely pink complexion!

LINDA'S BEST COLORS
- Cherry red
- Burgundy
- Black
- Icy white
- Royal purple
- Deep blue
- Silver
- Emerald green
- Pale yellow
- Fire-engine red

REDHEADS—*Earthy Tones Energize!*

Are you a redhead? "Red" hair runs the gamut from light copper to bright carrot to rich ginger. Red hair mixed with blond is known as "strawberry blonde." Red hair is the rarest hair color—and it can be devastating with the right colors!

Redheads usually sport very fair skin, which is inclined to freckle. Their eye colors range from soft blue to green to gray to a coppery brown.

Kim, our knockout redhead, looks for colors like tawny brown, forest green, misty yellow and soft blue—earth tones that pick up the colors of her hair and eyes give her the biggest boost. Kim even blends her red hair with blouses in pale red, but makes sure to stay away from all pink tones: They'll clash with her earthy looks! Black is a favorite color, because it dramatizes her flaming mane and accents her freckled skin.

KIM'S BEST COLORS

- Black
- Soft red
- Tawny brown
- Forest green
- Misty yellow
- Soft blue
- Soft gray
- Lavender
- Ivory
- Gold

★★★

Color also plays a part in *how you feel*. True! Want to feel calm and serene? *Wear blue*—it's the color of calm waters, deep emotion and loyalty.

Need a quick shot of confidence? *Wear green*—it's the confidence-builder and healing color, the color of trees and quiet glades. Think how well you'll be able to assert yourself wearing green!

On exam days at school, reach for your favorite yellows! Yellow—the color of sunshine—is said to stimulate your intellect! It also helps to make you more cheerful. So when you feel blue, *wear yellow*!

Are you feeling listless and want more energy? *Wear red*. Red is the color that raises your energy level and stimulates ambition. It is also said to make you feel more positive and outgoing—which is always important in making new friends and trying new activities!

When you're feeling slightly insecure—*reach for brown*! Brown is the color that represents home and hearth—it can offer comfort when your life is on the rocks!

Color is one of the basic elements in putting together a wardrobe. Choosing the best shades of your favorite colors will highlight your special coloring and make you look vibrant and lovely! Blondes in light pastels, brunettes in clear primary and secondary colors and redheads in colors close to the earth will light up every room they enter!

"The Look"—Which Is Best for You?

Well, you've figured out your own body type and chosen your best colors. Now it's time to investigate the look that's right for you.

Who do you think you are? Are you athletic? Are you artistic? Are you the romantic type—or more at home with rock 'n' roll? Or do you instinctively choose "classic" clothes that will look good twenty years from now?

Plugging into your "type" is the next basic step in assembling a wardrobe. To choose the look that's right for you, consider these questions:

- What is your lifestyle? Are you active, always on the go, swimming, biking, doing gymnastics? Or do you prefer to curl up with a good book when school is out?
- Are you very conscious and careful of the fabrics and styles you wear—or do you prefer clothes you can toss into the washing machine, whose generous cut will allow you to stretch and bend at will?
- Is it important to you to *make a statement* with your wardrobe? Do you like letting people know, just by looking at you, what kind of person you are?
- Would you prefer to own clothes that will look fashionable for years—or plug into the latest fads?

Answering these questions honestly is the first step toward determining your style. Let's look at the five basic types. Which one are *you*?

ATHLETIC

These are clothes for the "girl on the go." They're simple, loose and comfortable, often in one- or two-color patterns, in fabrics that allow the body to stretch and breathe easily.

The athletic type adores lightweight clothes that

give her the option of flexing and stretching her muscles to their fullest. She loves the feel of comfortable, easily washable fabrics, often cotton blends or synthetics. Her active lifestyle demands sturdy clothing, which can survive her endless softball games or dusty hikes in the woods.

Comfort and ease of movement are the athletic type's greatest considerations. If they are *your* greatest considerations, you're an athletic type.

ARTISTIC

The girl with a strong sense of individuality chooses the artistic look. These are the avant-garde clothes, featuring long flowing lines in both pants and dresses. These geometric designs are often echoed in the artistic girl's face—she may have an oval or heart-shaped face with a long, firm nose and pronounced jaw.

The artistic look is often the very modern look, as well. While other girls will stick to what's "safe," the artistic girl is first in fashion trends. Her clothes will be less fussy than many others, sometimes featuring nothing more than a dark skirt or leggings and distinctive shirt. The artistic girl will wear tomorrow's clothing today and revel in its stark simplicity. "Take me for what I am," the artistic girl says bluntly to the world. "I'm not going to change to suit you."

If you favor long, dramatic lines and simple but striking clothing, you're an artistic type.

ROMANTIC

The polar opposite of the artistic type, the romantic girl loves clothes with echoes of yesterday. She leans toward a super-feminine look, featuring soft colors and fabrics like lace, silk and velvet. Other girls might find it hard to keep such delicate fabrics in good repair, but romantics do not. Their indoor activities do not wear out their clothes nearly as quickly as the athletic types do. The styles they choose often emphasize soft, flowing designs and even an occasional ruffle, all reminiscent of styles women have been wearing for many years.

Romantic girls are the armchair adventurers. They prefer activities that are not very strenuous—they love to read, play or listen to music, paint, or write poetry and short stories. They often have a fascination with history, which gives them wardrobe ideas, and they're prone to daydreaming.

Because the romantic type is super-feminine, the lines of her clothes are much softer than the artistic type's. Romantic clothes emphasize a girl's curves and soften the angles to present the essence of timeless femininity. If you love soft, flowing styles and fabrics that play up your super-feminine side, you are a romantic type.

ROCK 'N' ROLL

The rock 'n' roll type is as contemporary as the romantic type is a fashion throwback. Rock 'n' rollers choose the latest—the flashiest—the *funkiest*—colors,

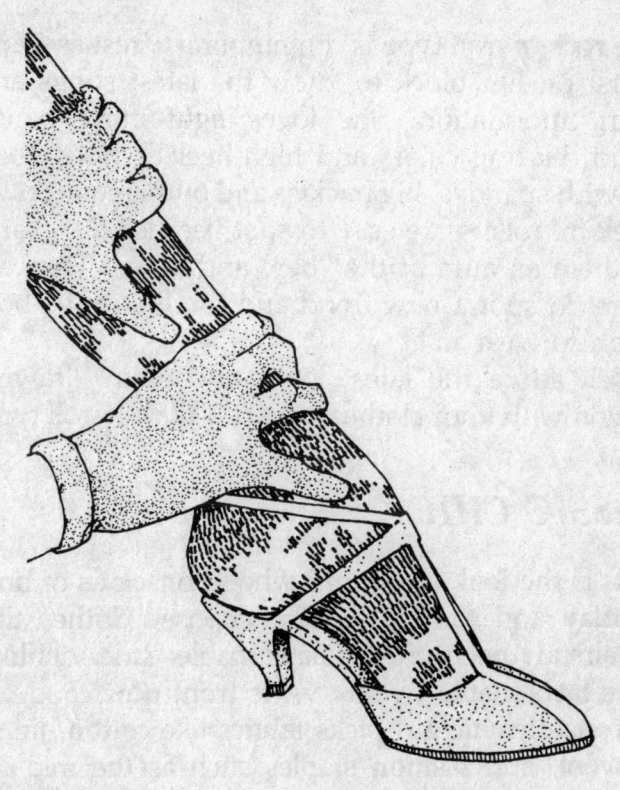

Mix and match—colors, patterns and styles—for fun!

fabrics and styles. They ride the trends for all they're worth!

Denim, wild sweat shirts, the latest skirt styles and *anything* leather are all in the realm of the rock 'n' roller. Their fashion statement is: *"Look at me!"* and to that end rock 'n' roll types mix and match crazy colors and styles. Often, they'll complete their outfits with wild boots, sparkly shoes, wacky jewelry and brightly-colored socks. If it looks like it can't be worn together, but it is—you can be sure a rock 'n' roller is wearing it!

The rock 'n' roll type is contemporary, restless, and the first on her block to know the latest songs and concert information. She loves tight-fitting pants, shirts in blazing colors and high-heeled shoes decorated with sparkles, big buckles and outrageous bows.

Rock 'n' rollers are easy to spot because they carry with them an aura of the "here and now." They are the first to spot a new trend and the first to be bold enough to wear it.

If *you* adore the latest looks and enjoy drawing attention with your clothes, you're a rock 'n' roll type.

CLASSIC CHIC

This is the look of the girl who's conscious of both yesterday and tomorrow. She chooses clothes that have already been proven fashionable—and will look just as fashionable twenty years from now!

The classic chic girl picks fabrics like cotton, linen, and wool, and fashion staples such as the mid-calf corduroy skirt, Shetland sweater and tweed blazer. Since these styles have flattered girls for years, the classic chic girl knows she can wear them with confidence. After all, this is a girl who means *business*!

Classic chic clothes are easy to spot. They're cut in trim, flattering lines, in fabrics with little or no synthetic content. Polyester and spandex have no place in the classic chic wardrobe.

Color is particularly important in the classic chic wardrobe. They will always be forthright and traditional. Classic chic girls will head straight for the blacks, navys, grays and beiges as their color base, and add flair with blues, reds and greens. There is no place in the classic chic wardrobe for hot pink, zebra stripes or wild multicolored blouses and sweaters. Keeping it simple and elegant is the key to classic chic.

If you're a girl who tends toward the more traditional styles, who approaches life in a straightforward, no-nonsense manner and chooses clothes to match, you're a classic chic type.

What about our fashion guides? What types are they?

Marcy, our lithe blonde, loves outdoor sports. She likes feeling light and comfortable in her clothes, and she spends too much time bending and stretching to be bothered with delicate, easy-to-soil fabrics. Therefore, Marcy is an athletic type. She enjoys the loose-fitting, easy lines of athletic-type clothes and the wonderful shades she can choose to complement her own fair coloring.

MARCY'S THREE FAVORITE OUTFITS

- A stretchy sweat suit in her favorite lilac.
- A flowing ivory skirt with a short-sleeved yellow cotton top.
- A pink jumpsuit in cotton and rayon that moves with her.

Linda, our dazzling brunette, loves clothes that echo other times. She's a romantic who reaches instinctively for fabrics like satin, delicate cotton and lace. Even the cut of her clothes suggests other times: She's the first to wear an old-fashioned, tight-fitting vest and traditional Scottish plaids.

LINDA'S THREE FAVORITE OUTFITS

- ✪ A white silk blouse with a lacy Victorian collar, and a plaid skirt that flares when she twirls.
- ✪ A cardigan sweater with embroidered flowers and a pair of pants.
- ✪ A deep blue and purple dress with elbow-length sleeves, accented with lace.

Kim, our fiery redhead, is a rock 'n' roll type. Contemporary, restless and alive to the world around her, Kim picks clothes that draw attention! She leans toward fabrics like leather, lace and cotton blends, and puts them together in wild combinations!

KIM'S THREE FAVORITE OUTFITS

- ✪ Black leather pants with matching jacket and black T-shirt with red-painted rock band logo.
- ✪ A miniskirt in forest green, topped with a lacy black camisole.
- ✪ Tawny brown leggings, and a sleeveless light blue top worn under an ivory oversized shirt.

☆☆ **FIND YOUR LOOK QUIZ** ☆☆

Answer the following questions about "the look" and how to find yours.

1. *If your lifestyle includes lots of reading, writing poetry and watching movies about historical events, you're likely to choose the _____ look.*

2. Being an individual is important to you. You choose clothes that fit your own uncompromising attitude. Therefore, you are a(n) _____ type.
3. You're always on the go, and your primary fashion concern is comfort. You are a(n) _____ type.
4. You choose to stick with simple but elegant fashions that have looked good for years. You prefer traditional to trendy. You are a(n) _____ type.
5. Keeping up with the very latest fashions is a big concern of yours. You love trying new trendy things. You are a(n) _____ type.
6. The _____ type is most likely to choose an outfit no one else would dare to wear—and she doesn't care what others say about her clothes as long as she likes them!
7. The _____ type is most likely to choose delicate, hand-washable fabrics for her clothes.
8. The _____ type is most likely to look for light, stretchy fabrics that are easy to launder.
9. The _____ type is most likely to buy a big sweat shirt emblazoned with the newest movie or television slogan.
10. The _____ type is most likely to borrow her mother's pearls for a night out.

Answers: 1. romantic 2. artistic 3. athletic 4. classic chic 5. rock 'n' roll 6. artistic 7. romantic 8. athletic 9. rock 'n' roll 10. classic chic

☆☆☆

Something Extra!

Now you've chosen terrific clothes based on your body type, best colors and personal style. But how do you s-t-r-e-t-c-h out those great outfits, so they cover your entire week? How do you make them look fresh and different every time you wear them? And how do you manage it all without wrecking your clothes budget?

The answer: ACCESSORIES. These special additions can dress up or dress down your basic clothing choices and give each outfit a new and distinctive look. With the right accessories, you can wear the same outfit again and again—and still hear compliments from your friends!

What are accessories? They're shoes, belts, scarves, gloves, any kind of jewelry (rings, bracelets, pins, necklaces, earrings, watches), handbags, pantyhose, socks and hats. It's your accessories that will really make a fashion statement—and are often the most fun part of your wardrobe!

Let's talk about different types of accessories—and how they can add zip to your wardrobe!

FABULOUS FEET!

Shoes are the accessory *everyone* wears. The right shoes can make all the difference—and you'll want at least four different types in your wardrobe:

FLATS FOR EVERYDAY COMFORT

The most comfortable and durable shoes in your wardrobe! The shoes you wear for casual times—as comfortable in class as they are after school! Classic chic and athletic girls will both enjoy loafers in dark brown or black. Classic girls will love the tasseled loafer's traditional look, while athletic girls appreciate the penny loafer's sturdiness and comfort. Rock 'n' roll girls might choose soft, ankle-high boots without heels, while the artistic girls will look for a synthetic-fabric flat in a geometric shape that is years ahead of its time. The romantic girls will like the skimmer, a super-feminine favorite from the 'forties and 'fifties, or ballet slipper flats.

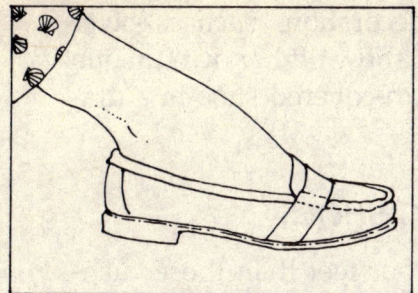

The Classic Loafer—always a good bet.

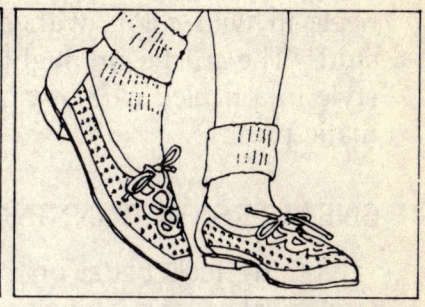

Dressy Flats—decorative and fun.

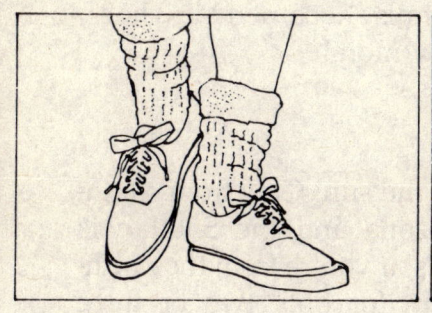

Sneakers—good for school and play.

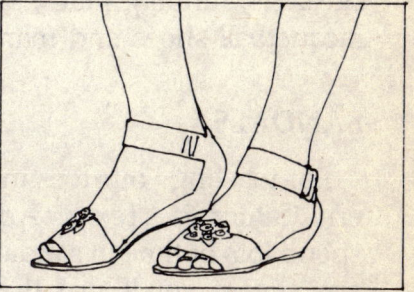

Sandals—summertime comfort and genuine style.

DRESS-UP SHOES

For those "special" times—the nights when you want to shine—you'll look for shoes in beautiful fabrics and colors to match your special outfits! Athletic girls will enjoy the ease and comfort of simple leather pumps, while romantic girls will choose high-heeled shoes in special fabrics like satin. The classic chic girl might pick a patent-leather shoe in traditional black, white or navy, while the rock 'n' roll girl will flaunt heels in wild colors with decorations such as silver studs. The artistic girl might show off her own unique style in a heeled clog or cloth-covered shoe in a dramatic print.

SNEAKERS OR RUNNING SHOES

Nothing feels better on your feet than those cushiony sneakers or running shoes designed for intensive workouts or Saturday morning chores! Choose from a variety of colors and specialties: everyone's favorite—sneakers, running shoes, tennis shoes, aerobics shoes, racquetball shoes and many more!

SANDALS

For toasting your toes in the sun! Girls from southern California, Texas, Arizona and the South will spend lots of time in sandals! If you're from the northern states, you'll use them for only two or three months a year—but they look *so* great with your beach outfits! You can choose from simple thongs, which are backless, or pick a sandal with a strap that encircles your ankle. Many sandals today are designed without a thong in the toe, which makes them far more comfortable for some girls to wear.

Sandals are made in many fabrics, ranging from leather to plastic to cloth to rubber. They come in every color of the rainbow—and often in wild prints!

To give your feet even more pizzazz, try a variety of brightly colored socks. Wear pantyhose in gray, black or sparkling ivory for more dress-up occasions, or knee-highs under those great jeans and slacks! And if you're looking to jazz up your favorite workout shoes—try sparkly shoelaces in hot colors!

☆☆ MAKING THE SHOE FIT QUIZ ☆☆

How do you know which shoes are best for you? Answer the questions below to determine the right shoe for the right look.

1. *If you're a romantic girl, you're likely to want a flat shoe like:*
    a. a penny loafer
    b. a skimmer
    c. a soft boot
    d. a geometric shoe
2. *If you're a rock 'n' roll type, your socks will be:*
    a. white ankle-length
    b. ribbed knee socks
    c. sparkly anklets
    d. sheer pantyhose
3. *If you're a classic chic girl, you might prefer a dress-up shoe in:*
    a. plastic
    b. leather
    c. printed cloth
    d. patent leather
4. *An artistic girl will show off her individuality in:*
    a. a unique clog
    b. a tasseled loafer
    c. a plastic high-heeled sandal
    d. a simple white running shoe

5. *An athletic girl will enjoy the comfort of:*
    a. ankle boots
    b. penny loafers
    c. patent-leather pumps
    d. plastic thonged sandals

Answers: 1. b; 2. c; 3. d; 4. a; 5. b

☆☆☆

BEJEWELED AND BEDAZZLING!

The most versatile accessory you can own is *jewelry*! Nothing livens up your look like rings, bracelets, necklaces or earrings! Just a few pieces can give you the perfect aura of classic chic, or show off your rock 'n' roll style. The artistic girl will choose special, "one-of-a-kind" pieces, while the romantic girl will pick more traditional jewels in settings that suggest the past.

RINGS

Show off your pretty hands with rings! You can find every kind of design imaginable—dramatic designs that extend down your finger, simple bands set with dazzling stones, or thin gold and silver interconnected rings!

If you have long, slender fingers, revel in the most outlandish rings you can find! But if you're inclined to shorter, stubbier fingers, pick rings that won't overwhelm you. You'll look glorious with one glittering stone!

Rings are a great fashion extra, because you can wear them in every mood and with every type of outfit. Shop around and mix and match to find the best look for you!

BRACELETS

Like rings, you can load up on bracelets to your heart's content! Pick one unique bangle that will enhance your wrist—or buy those sets of skinny plastic bangles in bright colors that jangle up and down your arm! Check out cloisonné, silver, and all kinds of wood and metal! You'll be amazed at what a bracelet, or a bunch of bracelets, can do for you!

EARRINGS

A fashion must! Earrings used to be strictly gold and silver and precious stones, but now they come in every kind of material for great fashion looks! There are round earrings, flat earrings, square or triangular earrings—or how about those love knots and hoops that never go out of style?

Girls with even wilder taste tend to wear earrings that dangle almost to their shoulders, in amazing colors and styles! Whether you have pierced ears or not, spend some time browsing at the earring counter—it'll be worth it to find the earrings that work best for you!

WATCHES

You don't have to wear them on just your wrist anymore! Watches come in a terrific variety of styles,

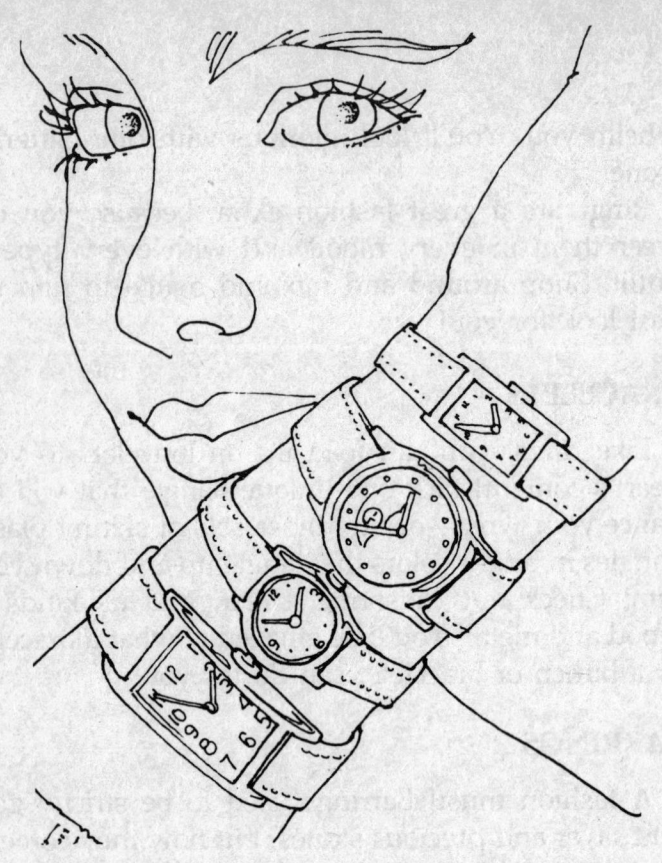

Watch Out! Group some watches together for the best time around.

and you can find almost anything that will suit you if you look hard enough.

More traditional girls can check out the watches with round, square or oval faces (in different colors) and black, brown or white leather straps! If you're an artistic type, you'll love to collect the new plastic watches with fabulous wild and geometric faces. If you prefer a bracelet to a band you'll find them in silver, gold and lots of different metals—and you can choose a loose- or tight-fitting bracelet to suit your taste!

Would you rather shake up your neighborhood? Look for the watches you can wear around your neck, as a necklace. Some of these are very modern and sporty looking, while other selections are old-fashioned and romantic. When you want to know what time it is—tip up the watch till you can read the face! They're decorative and exciting alternatives to wristwatches.

How about a watch as a brooch? Many smaller watches are mounted on pieces of metal or wood that you can pin right on your blouse! You'll be the envy of your friends—and you'll always know what time it is!

NECKLACES

A great way to dress up your outfit and draw attention to your pretty face!

Necklaces are available in as many styles, lengths and materials as you can possibly imagine. Show off your neck with a gold or silver or velvet choker—or let a long chain hang down to your belt! You can often buy necklaces in sets with matching bracelets and rings—or set your own fashion pace with one-of-a-kind pieces!

Traditional girls will own a set of pearls—while the artistic girl seeks her own voice with dramatic metal or fabric necklaces. As long as it loops over your neck—no matter what it's made of, how long it is or what it says to others—you're wearing a necklace!

PINS AND BROOCHES

What used to be Grandma's favorite piece of jewelry has become popular fashion for today's young woman, thanks to cool, new designs! You can find terrific brooches in today's styles, made of fake stones and backed with different types of metal or plastic. Wear them on blouses and sweaters—or pin them on your favorite scarf, belt or hat!

With a little imagination, you'll find great uses for brooches that tell people just how "today" you are!

Naturally, our fashion guides have their own favorite types and pieces of jewelry:

Marcy, our blonde athlete, likes jewelry that won't get in the way of her sporting activities—while still dressing up her clothes! She chooses tiny love-knot earrings and round, pink and black striped earrings to match some of her favorite outfits. She wears a pink-gold and yellow-gold ring on her long, slender hand—and pins a ceramic brooch onto her favorite scarf!

Linda, our romantic brunette, favors traditional jewelry. She loves the gold bracelet her grandmother gave her for her last birthday—and wraps a pearl choker around her neck to go with her favorite velvet dress! She, too, wears earrings—fake diamond studs when dressing up, and small dangling antique silver earrings for everyday.

Kim, our rock 'n' roll redhead, picks contemporary—often striking—jewelry. Her earrings dangle way down to her neck, and feature metals, bits of feathers and sparkling fake gemstones! Her favorite bracelet is a heavy, chunky piece of wood painted with black and red stripes, and she wears a wide strip of silver on her other wrist! She tops it all off with a silver collar at her throat.

HANDBAGS—*The Great Hideaway*

What can be more useful than that handbag you sling over your shoulder—or the backpack stuffed with a thousand essentials? Yet this "functional" accessory can be a real fashion extra!

Which do you prefer? Do you like the fashion "dress-up" feeling of a handbag—in soft leather or a sporty fabric? Shoulder bags come in different designs to fit your active lifestyle. You can dump everything into one big pouch—or tuck it into separate zippered compartments! And you can pick from soft leather, suede, cotton canvas or other fabrics. Swing it over your shoulder and look great!

Would you rather trade fashion for function and choose a backpack that can carry everything from books to workout clothes, to makeup and money? With heavily padded straps, backpacks are really comfortable for the long haul—a day of classes and after-school activities. Since backpacks are popular, you can find them in every color of the rainbow and in terrific exotic prints, too. Maybe you'd rather wear a tiny bag on a thin strap—a dressier, more elegant look if you're going on a special date or attending a big party. These bags are made of terrific leather or sparkly sequins—but they don't hold as much as your comfortable sports bag or backpack. You'll have to pack light to use one!

Picking the bag you'll love throughout the year is a matter of three factors: space, style and size. These are the best indicators as to which bag is really right for you.

Space is very important. How much do you want to carry with you? If the answer is "A lot"—then be prepared to pick a bag that can carry a lot! Choosing a tiny little square bag that looks great won't be much help when you try to stuff in three notebooks on top of a wallet, emery board, mirror and makeup! Be sure you know how much you intend to take with you on a day-to-day basis before picking a handbag.

Style is another crucial factor. If you're the more traditional and elegant type (classic chic or romantic), it makes no sense to buy a handbag that's sporty and casual-looking because it will clash with your style. On the other hand, don't fall in love with a wonderful, elegant-looking bag if you're the athletic type. Remember, your handbag has to match the style of the majority of your clothes if it's to contribute effectively to your total "look."

Size is the last crucial factor. If you're just five feet tall, will you look good with a giant-sized handbag? Or will your best friend, tall and broad, look right with a handbag that's scaled to a smaller girl? Check carefully before buying that super bag you're so crazy about. Look at yourself in a full-length mirror wearing or holding the bag. If the proportions seem right, go ahead and buy it! But if the bag either overwhelms you or seems far too small for your body—put it back on the rack and keep looking!

THOSE EXCEPTIONAL EXTRAS!

SCARVES

A great fashion extra! Long scarves in great prints, stripes, polka dots or other designs can make a world of difference. Twist a scarf around your ponytail. Wrap it around your slender waist. Knot it over your favorite hat—or tie it around your throat! Loop it around your dress so that it trails over your shoulders! It's the most versatile accessory of all—use it and love it!

BELTS

They not only hold up your pants and skirts—they can also keep your whole outfit from falling apart! Belts are available in lots of different fabrics and colors—from leather to canvas to twisted rope to colored elastics! Thread one through your jeans to match—or throw it over your favorite skirt to contrast! You can even loop it over a shirt—just for fun! Belts are the great put-together for complete fashion looks.

In buying belts, size is a major consideration. As with handbags, belts can overwhelm your body—or get lost in the shuffle. If you're petite and small-waisted, check out one- or two-inch belts in matching colors. If you're tall and long-waisted—pick up the widest, wildest belts you can find for contrast!

HAIR HELPERS

You can dress up your hair with super sequined combs—or tie it back with ribbons, barrettes, hair clips, or fabric-covered rubber bands!

Hair combs are super-feminine and come in a variety of styles. Check out the translucent tortoise-shell combs (dark and golden brown)—or pick up plastic combs in different colors! You can find combs decorated with sequins, flowers, feathers and silver studs—so pick your favorite for a super hair look! Ribbons, barrettes, hair clips and hairbands are also available in dozens of different styles, materials and colors. So dress up your glorious locks with the accessory of your choice.

How about our fashion guides? How do *they* accessorize their favorite clothes?

Marcy's pink jumpsuit becomes dazzling when she adds a colorful scarf in pink, black and ivory to tie around her slender waist! She pins back her blonde hair with tortoise-shell combs, so we can see her gold love-knot earrings!

Linda's traditional deep blue and purple dress becomes new and exciting when she adds blue ribbons to her dark hair—and belts purple velvet around her waist! With a gold bracelet dangling from her wrist and fake diamond studs in her ears, Linda looks very contemporary!

Kim's simple brown leggings, blue top and ivory oversized shirt get a boost in the accessory department! She ties a great printed scarf at her throat and throws on a wild leather belt over her shirt. With her stylish bracelets and the latest in rings—Kim is the girl for today!

★★★

DO's for Accessories
1. DO choose accessories in colors that match your clothes.

2. DO wear more than one bracelet, ring or scarf at a time.
3. DO choose accessories in styles that match your particular "look."
4. DO choose a handbag that reflects your lifestyle.
5. DO experiment with new ways to wear your terrific scarves!

DON'Ts for Accessories

1. DON'T mix accessories of one type with an outfit of another. (Don't wear romantic accessories with rock 'n' roll clothes!)
2. DON'T buy a handbag, no matter how great it looks, if its proportions don't match those of your body.
3. DON'T buy a handbag, no matter how great it looks, if it does not contain adequate space to carry *all* your stuff.
4. DON'T wear a large number of rings if your hands and fingers are small; the rings will make your hands look odd.
5. DON'T wear accessories of different types together (e.g., a rock 'n' roll handbag with classic chic earrings).

★★★

Accessories are the hidden power in your wardrobe. Nothing provides as much variety; nothing makes an outfit work better. Load up on accessories—you'll use them for years and love them forever! Choosing accessories wisely and using them well can turn your five-day wardrobe into one unending surprise after another!

Free and Easy Mood Dressing

We all know there's life after the last bell rings at school. And where there's life, there's—a change of outfit! Different occasions demand a different style of dress. But what to wear and when? Read on . . .

LOOKING GREAT WHILE WORKING OUT

Want to look good while you're *doing* good for yourself? Sure you do! And you can look fabulous in workout clothes designed to show off your figure while you're sweating off the pounds!

Check out those leotards—the foundation of a terrific workout look! Leotards are made in wonderful stretchy materials and glisten in a rainbow of colors. You can choose from sleeveless or short- or long-sleeved leotards, and boat-necked, scoop-necked, crew-necked or V-necked leotards. You can buy leotards in simple cottons—or wild synthetics! You can buy them with attached belts—and in stripes, polka dots or floral prints.

Blondes will pick leotards in light colors to match their own fair coloring. Brunettes will head straight for the boldest colors possible, while redheads will look for the earthy tones to play up their earthy looks!

Accessorize with super stretchy belts in wild colors—and add thick socks to match your belt! Naturally, under the socks (and leotard) you'll want to be wearing aerobics tights, which stretch when you stretch. They're made in shimmery colors from palest ivory to darkest black—and they give your legs a wonderful line!

And if you want to draw attention to your face—and keep your hair (and perspiration) out of your eyes—pick up some of those thick elastic sweatbands! Girls with long hair, particularly, will appreciate these terry cloth headbands which you can find in bright colors with stripes running through them—a great addition to your workout outfit!

Remember, no matter which outfit you pick—*always* lace on those super-comfortable aerobics shoes to complete the ensemble. Nothing is more important for preventing injuries!

Let the good times roll! Sporting clothes mean fun and sun, good health and great looks!

SPORTS DRESSING

How about *other* types of workouts—like organized sports? What do you wear to look spectacular—no matter what you play?

TENNIS

White is the color of all really terrific tennis clothes. You can play in short-sleeved or sleeveless tennis tops and in white shorts or skirts. You'll find tennis clothes in cotton, nylon and all manner of synthetics—so decide which fabric will keep your skin coolest and go for it!

SWIMMING

Your big decision here is—one-piece or bikini? If you want to smooth your body's lines or make yourself look taller, thinner or better proportioned, opt for the one-piece. If you're really crazy about your body and find a suit that fits just right—go for the bikini!

One of the terrific options you have with a bathing suit is the style of the neckline. You can buy a strapless suit and show off your gorgeous shoulders, a suit that has a neckline with two strings that tie in back, a tank-style suit with a scoop neck, or a high-necked suit with a low back. And there are lots of variations on those types!

After coming out of the pool, lake or ocean, you might want a cover-up in colors that match or contrast with your suit. Oversize, hand-painted T-shirts look terrific as cover-ups and so do short, terry cloth robes! Don't forget to slip on a pair of colorful rubber thongs to complete your look!

BIKING

It's hard and often uphill work, so you'll want to keep cool. Yet you're often biking in the blazing sun, so it's a good idea to cover those arms and shoulders that will be hunched over your bike! Try short-sleeved, light-colored T-shirts in cotton or a cotton blend. Light colors, after all, reflect the sun, while dark colors absorb it. You don't want to get any hotter than you're going to be anyway—and nobody wants to get a sunburn!

Add light pants or shorts. You might want to get a pair of tight stretchy biking shorts, available in sporting goods stores. These are usually made in dark colors and they are longer than conventional shorts, with greater flexibility of movement. Since they're designed especially for bikers, you can be sure they'll be comfortable—and you'll look like a biking star!

SKIING

The best sport you could choose to show off your growing fashion sense! Nothing looks as glamorous as terrific ski clothes! Sweaters are ski essentials. Pick long-sleeved, warm V-necks or crew necks in diamond, striped or print patterns—and under your sweater you can show off a turtleneck in a solid color! In extra-cold ski conditions, try a quilted vest in navy or stripes!

When choosing ski clothes, safety and warmth should be your first considerations. Luckily, there are gorgeous, waterproof outfits that offer both maximum protection and maximum fashion! So buy smart and look terrific!

Ski pants are made in different fabrics—nylon, stretch synthetics, heavy cotton blends—and many different colors. Bright colors are best for the slopes—

should you fall into the snow, bright colors will stand out.

Heavy quilted gloves, ski boots and goggles complete the skier's outfit. When you've put together a knockout ski outfit, you'll be the talk of the ski lift!

SOFTBALL

The easiest sport to dress for! Pull out your oldest cutoffs—your most faded sweat shirt—your favorite T-shirt—heavy socks and sneakers! Softball is a casual-dress sport—and you'll want to reach for the most comfortable clothes you own!

Shoes are the most important consideration here. Sneakers, running shoes and tennis shoes are all wonderful softball shoes.

For sitting on the bench, dress up your softball look with a casual sweater or sweat shirt tied over your shoulders—or around your waist! If you're keeping score and not playing, snap on some Indian silver and turquoise jewelry. And don't forget to slap on a baseball cap with your favorite team's logo on it!

CASUAL DATE DRESSING

You may not be ready for boy/girl dates yet, but how about great looks for casual group dates? Let's talk about how to look terrific when you attend:

FOOTBALL GAMES

Autumn games mean rich sweaters, bright jackets and super pants! If that cute guy is with your group, you'll want to show off your sporting attitude in the best fall colors available—bright pumpkin, earthy brown, golden yellow, dark leafy green.

Try a bright sweater with a scarf wrapped around your neck, under a corduroy jacket and matching pants. Or tuck the same scarf inside a white linen shirt and your best jeans, with an autumn-colored sweater over your shirt!

Football games are a great place to show off your very special suede pants and jacket—or a winter-weight jumpsuit!

CULTURAL EVENTS

Trips to museums, plays and ballets are perfect opportunities for those outfits you always considered "too good" for casual dates. This is a good time to wear that terrific silk shirt with your mid-calf-length skirt—or your best jeans with a lacy blouse and fancy vest.

Toss on those dazzling "too good for casual" accessories: the thin gold bracelet your grandmother gave you, hoop earrings, that very special hat, the jazzy little handbag you just can't use every day. They'll give you an added sophistication while you're enjoying a first-class performance or exhibit.

Whatever is "too good" for school and not quite dressy enough for formal occasions is the outfit you wear for a special cultural event!

MOVIE DATES

Girls' favorite nights out—and a great place for those easy clothes you feel so good in! Almost anything will look good at the movies—so it's up to you to decide how much you want to dress up—or down!

Jeans are a staple at the movies. Wear your most comfortable faded jeans with a T-shirt advertising your favorite rock group—and toss a short leather or jean jacket over your shoulder! Slip soft, well-broken-in jeans over your favorite long-sleeved leotard—and tie an oversized blouse over the whole thing! Or keep it simple with tight denims and your favorite V-necked sweater.

Jeans are the key to terrific movie-date dressing, but you may also wear casual pants (*not* sweat pants) with the combinations listed above. You're looking for a style somewhere between after-school and the Christmas formal. So experiment with your own jeans and pants combinations for wonderful, easy movie clothes!

INFORMAL DANCES

What a wonderful place to show off the clothes you wish you could wear all the time! Though they're called "informal," dances are still more special occasions than movie dates or football games—so trot out your best casual clothes for the evening!

Fabrics are the key here—if you own satin, silk or velvet clothes, try to find a place to use them in your informal dance outfit. A satin blouse and dressy skirt with heels, for instance, are perfectly acceptable at this kind of school function.

How about a dress that features a fancy belt or vest? Or a floor-length dress that isn't strictly a formal? For example, a white lacy top and long sweeping skirt would look great with heels and some of your better jewelry.

As a general rule, pants are more appropriate at more casual outings than at informal dances. Whether it's your first dance or not, you'll feel a lot more feminine dancing in a skirt that swirls around you. And a dance is the best place to show off those great legs—in colored or sparkly pantyhose!

PARTIES AT FRIENDS' HOUSES

Friends' parties run the gamut from super-casual to fancy dress—and it's best to check with your friend beforehand about the kind of party it's going to be. She (or he) can tell you what's expected and might give you an idea of what she (or he) will be wearing, so you can plan your own outfit accordingly.

If your friend says it's a casual party, plan an outfit similar to your movie-date clothes. If it's a little more dressy, look to your cultural-event clothes. If it's a fancy holiday or birthday celebration, you would be wise to lay out an informal dance type of outfit. Remember, it's important to feel comfortable at a party, so do your best to find out in advance what the dress will be. You'll be able to blend in happily and just have fun!

BIG DATE DRESSING

What about the *really* formal occasions? What do you wear to the super-formal dances, the New Year's Eve party, family weddings and the Christmas dance?

Stepping Out. Formal wear with a dramatic flair.

Nothing is more fun than dressing up! Both long and mid-length dresses, in lacy or shimmery fabrics, will make you glitter. And for these super-special occasions you can choose among silk, satin, taffeta, velvet, lace or crepe gowns that sparkle! Pull out those high heels, your favorite tiny satin purse, and hair combs decorated with lace and silk, rhinestones or pearls!

Whatever your favorite Cinderella fantasy outfit is—a formal occasion is the place to wear it! The dresses that make you feel like royalty are the perfect answer to the once-a-year bash or wedding of the century. Though your overall wardrobe will include only one or two fantabulous outfits . . . you'll dazzle everyone when you wear them!

Let's check out our fashion guides as they check out life after school!
Marcy, our blonde athlete, loves working out her fashion sense along with her body! For aerobics class she chooses a pink V-necked stretchy leotard, along with ivory-tinted stretch tights. She adds an ivory T-shirt—and coordinates with pink sweatband and pink socks that match the laces on her white aerobics shoes!
For a casual movie date, Marcy chooses to dress down, as do many athletic types. She slips on faded jeans with a pale yellow T-shirt—and ties her favorite pink sweat shirt around her shoulders! She prefers running shoes to anything dressier—and adds sparkle with the pastel scarf she wraps around her pretty blonde hair and ties in a soft bow.
For the super-formal occasions, Marcy still keeps it simple. Her floor-length lilac dress with thin spaghetti straps is cut like a tunic—straight down her slim figure—which accents her broad shoulders. She wears lilac-flowered combs in her hair and a silver choker at her throat. Her shoes are ivory leather with high heels.
Linda, on the other hand, displays her romantic style in all her outfits. Her bathing suit is a strapless floral print, and the colors play up her terrific eyes while the style shows off her curvy figure. She covers

the suit with a delicate cover-up that closes at her throat.

Linda, being an armchair adventurer, also *loves* cultural events, and always enjoys museum dates. Her favorite museum garb is a red blouse with a knee-length wool skirt and matching jacket. She tips a matching beret over her dark hair, and slips on medium-heeled black pumps. She finishes the ensemble with glittering ruby-stone earrings and her favorite ring.

Linda's romantic tendencies blossom at formal occasions! She digs out a floor-length deep burgundy velvet "Juliet" dress. At her throat she clasps on a pearl choker, and her shoes are her best black velvet slippers. Her ruby-stone earrings look great with the burgundy, and she pins back her hair with a burgundy velvet bow.

Kim, our redheaded rock 'n' roll type, keeps her contemporary look even in a softball game. Playing first base, she wears a black T-shirt with the logo of her favorite rock group and black nylon biking shorts. Glittery earrings dangle almost to her shoulders! To be sure she sees the batter's every move, Kim's wearing her 'fifties-style sunglasses outlined with sequins!

For parties at friends' houses, Kim stays in the rock 'n' roll mode. Her favorite casual party outfit is black jeans with a pale red shirt studded with rhinestones. She rolls up the shirt's long sleeves, and a silver bracelet inlaid with large, colored gemstones dangles at her wrist. Over the shirt she drapes her favorite denim jacket, collar turned up. She holds back her long red hair with sequined ribbons and slips her feet into soft kid boots. If anyone looks like "today"—it's Kim!

Formal occasions aren't really Kim's favorite times—but she manages to maintain her own style even then! Kim's preferred dressy outfit is a mid-length ivory satin dress with an off-the-shoulder neckline. The bodice is sprinkled with Kim's favorite glittering sequins, and coordinating sequins decorate the glittery clip holding back her hair. She wears ivory lace gloves and high heels—and still looks like the typical rock 'n' roller!

When the school bell rings, that's your signal to experiment with really creative new looks! Whether it's for sports, casual dates or super-special occasions, you can find a way to knock 'em dead with your own special style!

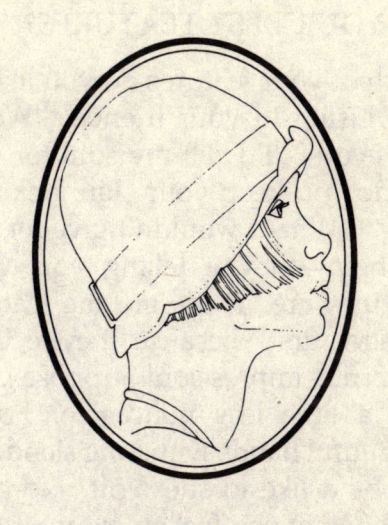

Show Off "The Best You!"

*E*veryone has her favorite features and they're the ones she wants to play up.

The best way to show off your good side is to develop a wardrobe that accentuates your best features. At the same time, it must downplay those tiny little imperfections we'd *all* rather forget we had.

PLAY UP YOUR GOOD POINTS

WHAT ARE YOUR BEST FEATURES?

Okay, which of your features do you like best? You don't know?! Listen to your friends: "Wow, you've got gorgeous eyes!" "I'd sell my soul for your waistline." "How do you keep your skin looking so fresh and beautiful?" "What I wouldn't give for your legs!"

Listen to them—they're telling you *exactly* what your best features are. Those are the features everyone *should* notice first—because they're the features that create a terrific impression! Suppose your beautiful areas are a little less noticeable? For instance, you've got beautiful hands with long slender fingers—or tiny hips you'd like to show off? No problem!

Make a list of what you feel are your best features—and check with someone else to be sure it's not just your own opinion. Do you have marvelous eyes—skin—hair—legs—shoulders—hands—feet?

Don't say you don't have *any* good features! *Of course* you do—everyone does. They may not be the features you wish they were—for instance, you might be ignoring your lovely skin while you were wishing desperately for a gorgeous figure—but don't ever put down your good points. Being able to see the good in yourself is essential in developing a fashion consciousness.

Okay now. Let's be honest. Look in that mirror and study your features. Figure out which ones really do make you feel best about yourself. Now ask someone else—someone who knows you well and will answer you truthfully. *You* think your eyes are super, but does your best friend think so? If she confirms it, you can be sure you do have terrific eyes. If she points out that you should be taking more credit for your pretty legs, think again. And pay attention to her compliments—and the compliments of your other friends. They'll tell you everything you need to know about your good points!

FOCUSING ON THE FABULOUS!

Now you're ready for the next step—what to do with those features to spotlight them effectively. Let's divide them into two categories: facial and figure.

Barrettes, combs, headbands—just a few of the fashionable accessories for your hair.

Facial features are any features completely separate from your figure. For instance, hair, eyes, skin, and ears are all facial features. Playing up these features depends mostly on the proper use of colors and accessories.

Beautiful hair looks even more attractive when you jazz it up with pretty hair combs, bows or barrettes. With blonde hair, use light-colored barrettes and bows—soft pink, powder blue, pale yellow—and the clearest tortoise-shell combs you can find! Dark hair glows under burgundy, electric blue or dark purple ribbons—and red hair gleams next to barrettes in forest green, rust or tawny brown!

Girls with long hair can be particularly creative. You can tie it into a ponytail—or let it swing free while you wear a satiny, bright-colored headband! Or take some time to braid cornrows—adding colorful beads for a terrific look! Very curly, frizzy, or kinky hair looks excellent when it's worn loose and curly with a zingy plaid headband. Choose the colors that look best with your beautiful hair—and watch heads turn!

Play up those gorgeous eyes with earrings, scarves and glasses! With light-colored eyes (blue, pale green, gray), choose big, fun earrings in soft colors to complement them. Dark eyes (dark blue or green, brown or black) sparkle next to dark green, deep red or blue earrings. Push your hair back so the stones show and wait for the admiring glances!

Scarves in the same distinctive colors mentioned above work beautifully to set off pretty eyes. And if you need glasses—good news! Glasses frame your eyes like beautiful pictures—so they look even more stunning! (And if you are farsighted your lenses will make your lovely eyes seem bigger!) Choose frames in light colors to set off light-colored eyes—and frames in dark colors to showcase dark eyes!

How about showing off your gorgeous skin? If you're proud of your creamy throat and shoulders—or your healthy, light tan—hang a necklace to emphasize those pretty areas! Dark olive or brown skin looks beautiful with silver jewelry. Wear a tank top to show off your arms and shoulders—or use earrings to accent your beautiful face! If your skin is very fair, use light-colored stones. If your skin is olive-colored, ruddy or dark, reach for the darker stones. What an amazing difference!

Pretty ears also need earrings—tiny love knots to show off your tiny ears or larger, more elaborate hanging earrings to go with a larger, beautifully-shaped ear. And don't forget to see whether a stud or a hanging earring looks more glamorous next to the shape of your face. With some attention to color and accessories, facial features can be bewitching!

Figure features encompass the entire range of your body: *neck*, *shoulders*, *waist*, *hips*, *legs*, *ankles*, *hands*, *feet*, *wrists*. Playing up figure features depends largely on the styles you wear. If your neck is long and lovely, use scarves, necklaces and special necklines to draw attention to it. Remember the importance of choosing the right colors—soft shades for pale skin, darker shades for darker skin—and experiment with every kind of bow and knot you can think of! Necklaces with large stones and big settings will look best against your neck.

- You can pick lots of different necklines to emphasize your *neck*. Emphasize its loveliness with a halter top—or lengthen it with a mock turtleneck (a short-necked version of the real turtleneck). Make it look even longer with a deep V-neck. The girl with the beautiful neck will revel in necklines—and for her, the sky's the limit!
- Have you got lovely *shoulders*? Choose off-the-shoulder necklines or wear halters to show off your bare shoulders—and wear bathing suits with no shoulders at all! Lacy peasant blouses are also a great look. You might even choose bracelets you can wear around your upper arm for further emphasis.
- Are you blessed with a tiny *waist*? Terrific—think of the wonderful clothes you can wear! Belts, sashes and dresses with tight waists are made for *you*! Choose outfits that cinch in at the waist.
- With tiny *hips* the same rules apply—but choose slacks that hug your hips and belt your clothes at the hip, not the waist.
- What if you've got beautiful *legs*? Lucky you! Invest in a large supply of bright tights in different colors—and keep an eye out for super-special shoes! You can also wear narrow pants and leggings—and the shortest skirts you can find! Choose clothes that will keep the lines long and slender—and you've got it made!
- If you have particularly pretty *hands*, be sure to play them up! Pretty hands will look even prettier in sheer gloves, or glistening with rings and bracelets! Choose blouses that flare at the wrists to attract attention to your hands—you'll be

amazed at the reactions you get! And remember to keep your nails well manicured!

✪ Enhance lovely *feet* with beautiful bare-looking shoes—particularly those that strap across the ankle! Keep a good supply of sandals—and you can add sparkle with a slender ankle bracelet!

For a hint of how it all works—let's look at our fashion guides!

Marcy, our athletic girl, is proud of her shoulder-length blonde hair, lovely long legs and broad shoulders. She emphasizes her good points with tortoise-shell combs in her loose hair—or blue and soft green ribbons with a long braid down her back! To show off her figure assets, she chooses a favorite halter top and adds a miniskirt. Her tights are brightly-colored and sparkly—completing the line of her great legs!

Linda, our petite brunette, particularly loves her dark, mysterious eyes. She pins back her dark hair so her ruby-colored dangling earrings call attention to her face. No one can miss those warm eyes . . . . Without further ado, she looks dazzling!

Kim, our rock 'n' roll redhead, gets compliments all the time on her lovely neck, beautiful skin and tiny waist. She makes it a point to pick a blouse with a flat collar—and adds a shimmery sapphire scarf that matches her eyes and further accents her neck! She emphasizes her pretty skin with huge sapphire earrings—and rolls up the sleeves of her blouse to show off the skin of her arms as well! And she makes her tiny waist look even tinier with a wide belt that she wears to finish off a great look!

CAMOUFLAGE YOUR PROBLEM AREAS

Well, great, you say. It's easy to show off your good points—but what about the other stuff? What do you do when you have features you wish you could change?

No problem! *Every* girl has features she would rather not have. The way to handle them is to find ways to de-emphasize them. What's your least-favorite feature? Do you have a thick waist—wide hips—bony knees—short, pudgy legs? Is your hair unruly—your skin blemished—eyes too small? No problem! Many face and figure imperfections are relatively easy to camouflage.

- If your waist is larger and your hips broader than you want them to be, wear dresses that fit loosely and flare out gently at the hem. You'll be able to show off your pretty face and legs instead of drawing attention to your waist and hips. You should also look for loose-fitting pants and avoid tight-fitting jeans. Choose lightweight materials that expand with you, such as cotton and linen. Fabrics like velvet and silk give less and tend to bunch up.
- Bony knees are easily covered by mid-calf skirts, pants or dark-colored panty hose.
- Short legs can be lengthened with high heels and clothes that emphasize a long vertical line. Slacks with hip-length jackets or simple knee-length dresses and skirts give the illusion of longer legs.

Dramatic, playful, flirty, casual—there's a hat for every mood and occasion.

✪ If your hair is unruly, hold it back with a colorful scarf or pretty barrettes. Pulling back your hair from your face into a ponytail tied with a bright ribbon is a wonderful way to give your hair the illusion of control—or tuck it all under your favorite hat!

✪ Eyes that you think are "too small" can be enlarged with a little eye makeup. Dangle large earrings that complement your eye color and see how your eyes seem to grow!

STRIPES AND POLKA DOTS—A FASHION WEAPON!

Stripes and polka dots are very effective fashion tools—when you know how to use them properly. Use them to emphasize—and use them to slim!

Stripes are a great help in giving the illusion of height—or seeming to add curves where there are none. Vertical stripes (stripes that run up and down an outfit) can make you look taller and slimmer and give longer lines to your body. Petite girls—or girls who want to hide a weight problem—will benefit from wearing vertical stripes. Horizontal stripes (stripes that run side to side) give a feeling of fullness to the body, which is helpful to the girl who dislikes her lack of natural curves. Thin girls or girls who have not yet developed will appreciate the illusions created by horizontal stripes.

Polka dots are a terrific "look-at-me!" item in your wardrobe. Large polka dots look best on taller girls, while smaller polka dots are better scaled to smaller girls. Use polka-dot accessories to highlight your favorite feature—but be sure *not* to wear them around a feature you're less than enchanted with! For instance, if your waist is large, don't wrap a polka-dot belt around it. It will only seem larger than it is. Polka dots are for the parts of you that you love *best*!

✰✰✰

Let's see how our fashion guides handle their "problem areas":

Marcy, our tall blonde, dislikes her lack of curves. She wears bold horizontal stripes to add fullness to her body—and avoids tight-fitting sweaters that would emphasize her chest! To draw attention from her bust, she wraps a polka-dot belt around her waist and fluffs out her hair around her shoulders. Her blouses and jackets are loose, not snug, which adds extra fullness where she needs it most.

Linda, our romantic brunette, has a tendency to put on weight at her waist and hips. She chooses sleek A-line skirts to draw the eye away from these areas and wears vertical-stripe skirts whenever possible! Her fabric choices tend to be expandable materials that will breathe with her body instead of constricting it.

Kim, our rock 'n' roll redhead, tends to have frizzy hair, particularly in humid weather. To deal with this, she often pins back her red curls and wraps them in a scarf—or simply uses combs and barrettes. Kim is very fond of crazy hats, as well—and hats keep her hair out of her eyes and in order, while giving her a terrific and "different" look!

☆☆ LOOK YOUR BEST QUIZ ☆☆

How do you play up or play down your best—and worst—features? Choose the one best answer for the following questions:

1. *You're proud of your pretty eyes and want to show them off. Therefore, you choose:*
    a. jangling bracelets
    b. sparkling earrings
    c. a studded belt.

2. *You're a head taller than all your classmates, and you want to de-emphasize your height. So you pick:*
   a. vertical stripes
   b. black leggings
   c. horizontal stripes.
3. *Your hips are tiny and terrific, and you want to show them off. Therefore, you:*
   a. wrap a belt around your waist
   b. tie a scarf around your hips
   c. slip on your tightest shorts.
4. *What's the best way to showcase your long, slim legs?*
   a. skinny pants
   b. an ankle bracelet
   c. a tight-fitting sweater.
5. *Wearing vertical stripes is a wonderful way to:*
   a. look fuller and more curvy
   b. show off your favorite feature
   c. look taller and slimmer.
6. *Facial features include your:*
   a. waist
   b. skin
   c. feet.
7. *Figure features include your:*
   a. hips
   b. eyes
   c. nose.
8. *Polka dots are a perfect way to:*
   a. give your body slimmer lines
   b. emphasize your best features
   c. make your body look more petite.

9. *Scarves are effective in accenting your:*
    a. shoulders and skin
    b. legs and wrists
    c. neck and eyes.
10. *An excellent method of deciding on your best features is to:*
    a. compare them with pictures of fashion models
    b. ask friends and family to point them out
    c. decide without counsel and dress according to your own feelings.

Answers: 1. b; 2. c; 3. b; 4. a; 5. c; 6. b; 7. a; 8. b; 9. c; 10. b

☆☆☆

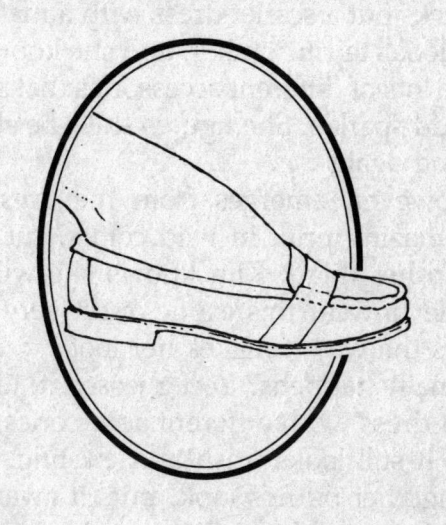

When the Going Gets Tough...the Tough Go Shopping!

SHOPPING SMART

*A*rmed with newfound knowledge about their own best colors and styles, *Linda* and *Kim* set off for the local mall together. They're looking for some knockout clothes for an upcoming school dance.

Linda picks out a scarlet dress with a matching belt. The color looks terrific on her, and she knows she'll be able to use lots of different accessories that she already owns to add sparkle. She figures she'll be able to wear it again and again . . .

Kim, however, emerges from the dressing room with an amazing print in wild colors, cut on a slant straight up her thigh. Kim knows she will probably not be able to wear this exotic outfit very often, but she adores the way it makes her look . . .

What finally happens? You guessed it. Linda wears her scarlet dress, with different accessories, for over a year, and it still looks fresh and exciting. Kim, who can't change her outfit's look, puts it away after one wearing. It's too wild for most occasions and tough to accessorize. She got stuck with a one-time outfit because of bad shopping habits.

Before you can wear a great new look, you've got to shop for it—and shopping can be great fun . . . or a great hassle! Let's talk about how to shop to maximize the pleasure—and minimize the pain, both to your mental health and your pocketbook!

SHOPPING WITH MOM—FUN OR FRANTIC?

She knows you better than anyone else. She may have more patience with you than any of your friends do. After all, she's been dressing you since you were little. But she still thinks you're her baby. It's time to show her how grown-up you really are!

For instance: You spot a super outfit and try it on—and it looks just great! But Mom picks up something she thinks is "so sweet"—and you know you'd rather die than wear it! What to do?

The key is to stay calm. If you throw a tantrum, your mom will think you're still a child—and she may be right! You have to show her that your objection to her choice is based on reason, not childish temper. You might explain that the outfit is very nice, but you feel you've outgrown that style—or that, based on your own careful study of your type, it won't work with the rest of your wardrobe.

Sometimes you'll find that you can work *with* your mother on clothes choices. For instance, she thinks that rust-colored jacket is so suitable, because it "goes with everything." But rust is not one of your best colors—you'll look much better in the same jacket if it's in burgundy. Yet you also believe the jacket would be a wise purchase.

Show your mom the two jackets, holding each up to your face so she can study the color. Explain how you arrived at your conclusions about your own coloring and what works best. Remind her that you *agree* with her that the jacket will look terrific in your wardrobe—you can wear it in school, after school, on casual dates, on weekends—but you will feel more comfortable in a color that enhances your own coloring.

How about accessories? Mom picks up a gorgeous scarf that she wants you to wear around your neck. But you know that your neck is too small—the scarf will look as though it's tying your head to your shoulders!

How about wearing the scarf as a headband? Or tying it around your ponytail? Maybe it would look great threaded through your jeans, as a colorful belt—or wrapped around your favorite hat!

Or Mom surprises you with the gift of a sweater—

that you *really* don't want to wear! Perhaps it has a round collar, when you prefer V-necks, and you know it won't do anything to enhance you. So tie it over your shoulders! Wrap it around your waist! Mom will be pleased that you're wearing her gift—and you'll be minimizing its impact on your total look.

What happens if Mom chooses an item you know you just can't live with? No matter how you try to explain it, she refuses to listen. That's the time when you must put your foot down—politely and reasonably. Do *not* say, "Mom, I hate that outfit, and you have terrible taste!" This approach is not likely to help matters and will hurt her feelings. Instead, point out to your mother that you really do not agree with her choice. In the long run, it will be a waste of money, since you will not wear the outfit. Most mothers are very budget-conscious, so she'll see the wisdom in not forcing the purchase.

On the other hand, your mother may be a very enthusiastic and flexible shopper who *loves* spending time at the mall with you. Enjoy this special time together with Mom!

SHOPPING WITH A FRIEND

It can be the best way to spend an afternoon with someone you really like. What could be more fun than comparing the latest styles and choosing new clothes together? But shopping with a friend can be full of hidden pitfalls . . .

Marcy and *Linda* are shopping for that perfect outfit for the beach. Marcy chooses a pink bikini that looks wonderful with her super figure. But Linda, with her petite, curvy figure and dark hair, won't look nearly as good in the bikini.

When Marcy presses her to buy it—"Won't it be fun wearing the same suit?"—Linda has to decide how to deal with her. Does she say yes to avoid hurting Marcy's feelings, or does she say no and rely on her own judgment?

It's important to listen to your own sense of style in shopping with a friend. It's easy to forget all the rules you struggled to learn when your best friend says, "Hey, that would look great on you!" She may be right—or she may be wrong. Be sure you check the prospective purchase against the rules you've learned about style, color and type before rushing to the cash register!

Don't be in a hurry to wear the identical clothes your best friend buys. It may look super on her but not nearly as good on you! On the other hand, you may look wonderful in the same styles—but be sure to choose a color that works well with your coloring. Softer colors look great on Marcy, but richer, intense colors are a much better choice for Linda.

You must also *watch your budget carefully* when shopping with a friend. It may be okay for her to buy a dozen outfits, but the same kind of spending could wreck *your* clothes allowance! Be sure you decide before you start exactly what you can afford to buy on this little excursion—and then stick to that decision! If you intend to look for one sweater, don't get involved in trying on beachwear! You'll resent it when you can't buy that terrific bikini you've been modeling in the dressing room. Or worse, you'll buy it, ignore the sweater you really need, and end up not wearing your "impulse purchase" at all.

Your friend is usually sincerely interested in helping you look terrific—but she may not know as much about personal style as *you* now do! Or she may be influenced by colors and styles she particularly likes—whether they look good on either of you or not! Be friendly but firm in refusing help that's detrimental. "Thanks for the input, but I like the blue," is a nice way to let your friend know that you like to hear her opinion—but *your word* is final. Your friends won't be hurt—in fact, they'll admire the way you know exactly what's right for you!

SOLO SHOPPING

Sounds like a drag, doesn't it? Who wants to shop alone, when you could be giggling and comparing outfits with a girlfriend? And who wants to face all those salespeople without back-up?

Think again. Shopping alone can often be the most rewarding way to pick your wardrobe. There's no peer pressure and no chance of an argument with your mother. You're free to zero in on the fundamentals of smart dressing and make wonderful choices!

As with any shopping, there are points to be aware of. Above all, when you're spinning through a rack of clothes, be sure to:

- *Read labels.* You'll want to check the size on the garment's label. A store tag may say it's an 11, but if the garment label says it's a 9, you can be sure it's a 9! Labels list the garment's size, style, fabrics and country of origin. (In the United States, labels also contain cleaning instructions.) You'll save yourself time and trouble if you read labels before you buy.

- *Know what fabrics you're buying.* It's important to know what fabrics comprise that slinky number you're dying to buy! Suppose there's acrylic in the fabric and you're allergic to all acrylics? What if your new blouse is all silk? Silk is beautiful to touch, but stains do not scrub out easily, and the fabric may unravel after many hard wearings.
- *Read cleaning instructions.* Suppose the label says "Hand wash only"? If you're responsible for your own laundering, you may want to reconsider buying a garment that will take lots of time to care for properly. And labels that say "Dry clean only" mean it. Do you want to spend part of your allowance every month on dry cleaning?
- *Buy wash and wear most often.* Wash and wear clothes are the sturdiest to wear and the easiest to care for. When they're dirty, you toss them in the washing machine, then in the dryer (or in some cases over a drying rack)—and in a few hours you have clean clothes! If you detest ironing, you'll love wash and wear—clothes made of wash and wear fabrics can often skip the ironing board altogether!
- *Check the garment for imperfections.* Once you've made up your mind that the size, color, style and label instructions are right for you, examine the particular garment carefully before taking it to the cash register. Are there snags in the fabric? Is the hem unraveling? Is there a dye blotch on the

front? Are the seams firmly sewn together and all buttons securely on the fabric? You'll want to buy a garment in the best condition possible, so be sure to look it over *before* you take it home. After all, if you're paying for a brand-new, perfect garment, that's what you should get!

NO NEED TO BLUSH

How about those "unmentionable" purchases—like a new bra? You know you have to get advice from the saleswoman—but how do you approach a perfect stranger when you don't even like discussing this with your mother?

Relax. Sales personnel in lingerie are trained to fit you quickly and expertly. When you're buying a bra, the saleswoman will ask your size. If you are not sure (most young women fluctuate in bra sizes for several years), the saleswoman will fit you.

Using a tape measure, she will measure your width, drawing the tape around your upper ribs. The number she reads off is the inch measurement you'll look for on a bra label—28, 30, 32, 34, 36, etc. Should your width measurement be an odd number, the saleswoman will recommend a bra sized to the next highest number.

For your cup size (the letter designation on the bra label), it's best to try on various cup sizes. The one that fits you best while giving you ample room in front and at the sides is the cup size you should wear.

Saleswomen will show you a variety of bra styles in your size, and you must *always* try on a bra before buying it. Bras and underpants, like bathing suits, are nonreturnable items, so you will want to be sure that the bra you choose is really what feels best to you.

You can choose from bras with stretchy straps or adjustable ones, bras that close in front or in back, padded or non-padded bras, bras that contain an underwire (as a kind of uplift) or those without. Remember, *you'll* be wearing it, so be sure the size and style are comfortable for you!

SALES!

What a temptation! Girls who are normally sensible can go stark raving mad at store sales! After all, if you wanted it when it cost $60, how are you going to resist when it's marked down to $30?

Sometimes, girls, you just have to. You may admire a knockout satiny prom dress—but if you're shopping in November, it won't really be worthwhile. Even on sale, will you be getting your money's worth if you buy it? Or will it simply hang in the closet because you haven't got any place to wear it? Remember, if it didn't suit your lifestyle and body type at its original price, why should it fit any better when it's on sale?

On the other hand, sales are a great way to stock up on items you would normally have bought at regular prices. Your favorite underclothes are a bargain at lingerie sales, and you can often pick up T-shirts, jeans, sweat shirts and a variety of sporty clothes at great sale prices. Just remember that often sale items are not returnable—so be sure that what you buy is what you'll wear!

SALESPEOPLE WE ALL HAVE KNOWN

Sales personnel can be the toughest nuts to crack when you're shopping! It's true that some can be great, but some can drive you *crazy*. Have you ever met the salespeople listed below?

"Ms. Aloof": She treats your mother wonderfully, but she's not nearly as gracious toward you. In fact, you suspect she'll try to correct your manners if you stick around long enough. Her clothes selection is usually high-priced but elegant, and she doesn't think you have any taste, so prove her wrong! Keep your questions simple and to the point, and don't allow her superior attitude to push you away from your shopping fundamentals! Above all, don't try to get on her good side—she doesn't have one!

★★★

"Ms. Pushy": She's working on commission, so she doesn't get paid unless you buy. That means she'll practically throw a rope over you when you step into the store and hurl you into a dressing room!

She's also likely to push you into a purchase that may not work for you at all. Don't trust her taste. Since she's eager to make a sale, you can't rely on her opinions. Remember, she'll tell you you look gorgeous in that burlap sack no matter how ghastly you really look—so be on your guard! The best way to get her off your back is to tell her you're just looking.

★★★

The Gossip: You'll adore talking to her, but if you're not careful, you could be saying "I'll take it" without knowing what you've bought! The Gossip gets to you by engaging your attention about everything but clothes. You're likely to get a rundown of everyone she knows, but you won't get much help with the items you're looking at. The Gossip hasn't got time to develop a fashion sense: She's too busy being the Town Crier. If you don't tune her out—politely, but firmly—you may end up buying a fashion disaster simply because you're distracted!

★★★

The Grandmother: The Grandmother's usually very sweet, but you can guarantee that she won't be up on the latest styles. She's probably never heard of spandex. You have to suggest to her, gently, that you'd like to pick your own clothes. If you don't, you're liable to end up with a closetful of hoop skirts!

★★★

The Gem: The rarest of the group—and if you find her, hold onto her! You can ask her any fashion question and get sensible, highly creative answers. She knows how to fit you so you look fabulous and often takes the initiative in putting together outfits you'll adore! She can even suggest specific accessories that will jazz up the simplest clothes and make you a standout!

She's ethical, too: If an item doesn't look great on you, she won't let you buy it. And she won't show you anything you can't afford. If you meet her, get her name and phone number *immediately*!

★★★

DO's for Smart Shopping

1. DO trust your own inner voice when choosing clothes. By now you know yourself well enough to know what looks good and what doesn't!
2. DO decide what you need and want to buy *before* a shopping trip—and stick with that decision no matter how tempted you might be!
3. DO stay calm when your mother chooses an item you hate—either you can minimize the problem by choosing it in another style or color, or you might be able to use it as a special accessory. If all else fails, tell Mom you just won't wear it.
4. DO read labels carefully so you know exactly what you're buying. Watch out for delicate, hand wash or dry clean only fabrics; buy wash and wear most often.

DON'Ts for Smart Shopping

1. DON'T buy a bra without help from the appropriate sales personnel. Fit and comfort are all-important, and bras are nonreturnable once they're purchased. Take the time to be fitted correctly, and feel free to ask any questions you have. The sales staff is there to serve you.
2. DON'T buy at store sales unless you're shopping for items that will fit into your wardrobe as a whole. Beware of "impulse purchases" that you won't really use. Use sales to stock up on items

you always wear such as underwear, jeans and T-shirts.
3. DON'T allow pushy salespeople to influence you into buying an item you know you won't wear. Sales staffs can be persuasive, but your own good sense should prevail at the cash register.
4. DON'T allow your friends to pressure you into buying an item that may look great on them, but won't look as good on you. You are ultimately responsible for your own wardrobe, so you should be careful at all times when shopping with your friends. Remember, when you know what you're looking for, shopping can be fun!

★★★

Recycling

What happens if you *can't* go shopping when you want something new? You're sick to death of the same old wardrobe, but you can't afford to check out the stores—and you don't sew well enough to make new clothes! What do you do?

Just when you think you'll never be able to manage a new outfit again—presto! You remember the closet full of old clothes that no one bothers to look at anymore. At first glance, it may seem useless, but if you put your imagination to work, you can develop a whole *new* look based on these forgotten goodies.

Mix up the old and you've found a bold new look.

COORDINATING NEW OUTFITS OUT OF OLD CLOTHES

✪ Pull that old eyelet blouse out of your closet—the one you're embarrassed to wear because it looks babyish with its puffed sleeves and round collar. Okay, let's make it look cool—take your favorite faded jeans, throw the blouse over it, add a bright belt with silver studs. Put on some wild accessories—and suddenly you're the hottest dresser in town!

- Instead of tossing your old skirt in the garbage or tearing it up for cleaning rags, an artistic girl like yourself can create a dynamite look by adding a pair of tights or leggings in a dark color under the skirt, and a blazer over that! Toss on a belt and some silver jewelry—and presto! From boring to bewitching, without spending a cent!
- Usually, the trick to blending new clothes with old is in matching colors that will mix well. Your old red shirt, for instance, will look terrific with a gray skirt, plaid pants (if the plaid includes red) or red shorts! (Make sure your reds blend and don't clash with each other.)
- How about denim? You've got a dark denim jacket and a very light denim skirt. How to wear them together? Easy—take the time to bleach out the dark denim until it (almost) matches the light skirt. They'll look great together and your friends will think you spent the weekend shopping!
- Wearing old clothes *differently* is another great wardrobe-stretching trick. If you always wore your purple sweater over a shirt, but it's a little worn now—tie it over your shoulders! Roll up the sleeves of your shirt and dangle a bracelet or two at your wrist—and you'll look new and fresh! Or that white shirt you wore to death that now looks a little ragged around the edges? Don't tuck it in—take the ends and knot them together! And if you roll up the sleeves, no one will see the stain on the cuff!

Your coordinating need not be limited to your own clothes, either. Perhaps your mother or older sister have items they no longer wear. *You* can wear them (if the colors and styles work with your coloring and type) and look just great! Remember, what was fashionable years ago usually comes back into style if you wait long enough!

- ✪ Try your sister's oversized blouse—only *you* can wear it as a dress, with ribbed tights underneath and lots and lots of your favorite jewelry to dress it up! How about your mother's discarded scarf? If you're the artistic type, swing it around your neck and fasten it with your favorite pin, so that it shows under your shirt. If you're a romantic, pull back your hair and tie the scarf over your ponytail—or wear it as a belt if it's long enough!
- ✪ Your father and brother can also contribute to your wardrobe. Those dress pants your brother outgrew two years ago are just about your size—and rolled up from the bottom and pulled tight with a leather belt, they'll look as good on you as they did on him!

Coordinating new outfits with old clothes is limited only by *your* imagination. Also, don't forget to ask first before raiding closets at home! Remember, every garment you own can work in many different ways. If you take the time and trouble to try new combinations, you can stretch your wardrobe to include outfits you never dreamed of!

JEWELRY

You'll be surprised at the wonderful new jewelry you can make yourself—if you really look around your house for suitable materials. You don't need to have spare diamonds lying around in order to come up with some eye-catching accessories!

EVERYTHING OLD IS NEW AGAIN

Think about all the jewelry your family has set aside in the last few years that they have no intention of ever wearing again! Those discarded pieces can turn into super "new" jewelry for you—if you keep your eyes open!

For instance, Dad's old cuff links can make terrific earrings, with a little alteration! See your friendly local jeweler for advice on removing the "link" and adding the apparatus to change cuff links into earrings for pierced or non-pierced ears!

Old necklaces of bright costume jewelry can be carefully taken apart, and the sparkling "jewels" used as studs on your denim jacket—or glued to a thin piece of metal or plastic to become glittering hair barrettes! If you really loathe that old costume ring your sister passed down to you two years ago, take the stone out of it—and set it into a piece of bright gold-colored metal to make a jazzy brooch!

After all, nothing *has* to remain as it is—if you can find a better way to wear it!

DULL TO DAZZLING

What about jewelry you can make from scratch? Well, okay, you say, sounds kind of interesting—but what do I use for material? Look around your house! Everything you'll ever need is right in front of you. Ordinary thread, ribbons, sea shells, and different-sized beads can help you make heads turn!

Let's talk about—earrings! Now is the time to do something with all those great shells you collected at the beach last summer. Make wonderful shell jewelry by keeping the shells in their natural form, or paint them your favorite color. Once the paint is dry, you can glue on a tiny earring back at the top of the shell, near the center. These earring backs are available in kits at hobby shops and five-and-dime stores. If you want to get even fancier, you can cover the shell with sequins. Put a tiny drop of glue on the shell with a pin, then use the pin to edge the sequins over the glue. This takes time and practice, but you'll end up with some great, glittery earrings!

Those same shells, or anything that will fit on a string, can become necklaces and bracelets, too! Drill or poke holes in each piece if you need to, thread a needle with colored or metallic thread, and string on your choice of beads, buttons, shells or whatever! (Narrow elastic is an excellent substitute for thread—it will stretch over your hand or head and fit closely at your wrist or throat.)

Ribbon dipped in rubber cement and mounted with tiny beads, gems or sequins can make dynamic rings or bracelets—even hair ribbons!

There's no limit to what you can create! Look

around at what's available to you—then let your imagination soar! Whatever the family discards—whatever you find in an exploration of your kitchen or family room at home—can turn into beautiful, unique jewelry you can enjoy for years.

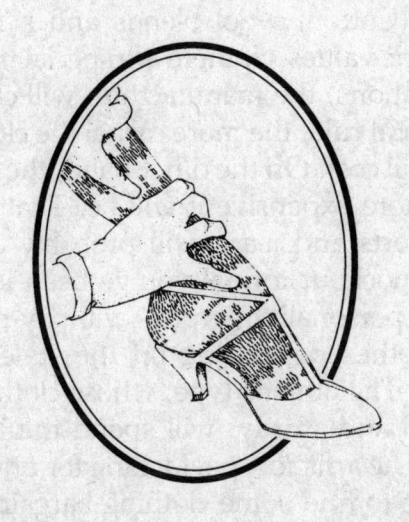

Fashion Smarts

Now you know the fundamentals for choosing the clothes that will look best on you. How about the other BIG question—how much will it cost?

Aside from how good it looks on you, your greatest consideration will be how well a particular item fits into your budget. After all, almost none of us has unlimited money to spend on clothes. So we have to learn to get the most out of our clothing dollars.

Many factors affect the price of a garment. If it was made by a famous designer or company, it will usually cost more. If it's made of unusual or delicate fabric, like silk, satin or suede, it will tend to be very expensive. (Cotton, wool blends and synthetics are the best fabric values.) If there are special trimmings or style innovations, the manufacturer will charge extra.

As a general rule, the more casual the clothing item, the less it will cost. On the other hand, the dressier the item, the more expensive it will be. That means that T-shirts, shorts and jeans will probably cost far less than that knockout formal you've been looking at!

Different personality "types" will pay more or less for their clothes depending on the styles they'll be looking for. The athletic type, whose clothes are most often casual and sturdy, will spend the least on her wardrobe. The artistic type, looking for unusual items, may be able to find some clothing bargains. The rock 'n' roll type will buy more to assemble each outfit, but the various pieces she buys will be contemporary and mostly inexpensive. The romantic and classic chic types can expect to pay the most for their clothes—they'll be seeking out special fabrics and classic styles, which tend to make their wardrobes the most expensive. However, the clothes will probably last longer and will not go out of fashion quickly.

To make life easy, we suggest that most girls stick to this simple wardrobe plan:
- School clothes—70% of wardrobe
- Casual clothes—15% of wardrobe
- Fashion "extras": Bathing suit, sunglasses, beach robe, running shoes, accessories—10% of wardrobe
- "Dressy" clothes—5% of wardrobe

SCHOOL CLOTHES

You need at least five basic outfits—or pieces you can mix and match for five school days per week! If your school dress code is flexible, you may be able to toss in some of your casual clothes—such as sweat shirts, jeans and tennis shoes—or you may want to keep your school clothes completely separate.

- If you keep them separate, you'll want to own about four blouses, three or four sweaters, two or three skirts, two pairs of pants, and two dresses exclusively for school use. If you live in a warm-weather climate, you can cut down on the number of sweaters you'll need—or if your home state is cold for half the year, you may want to add one or two additional sweaters.
- *Blouses* or *shirts* will vary in cost, depending on whether they are long- or short-sleeved and what fabric they're made of. Wash and wear fabrics will be less expensive than silk or satin, so they're a good choice for everyday wear. But if you want one really elegant blouse for special occasions, buy silk or satin!
- *Pants* and *skirts* can often be bought inexpensively, if you know exactly what you want and plan to buy mostly classic styles in solid colors made from washable fabrics. Often you can find these items on sale or in discount shops, and wear them for more than one season.
- *Dresses* can be expensive, since they often include in the price a special belt, vest or other item designed especially for that dress. Finding those one or two perfect school dresses can absorb a large part of your "school clothes" budget.

T-shirts are a girl's best friend!

CASUAL CLOTHES

You can go far on very little in buying basic jeans, T-shirts and other sit-around-the-house items. These are the items you can ideally pick up at flea markets or factory outlet stores for half the price a department store would charge—so it's worth shopping around a little! "Casual clothes" items include *jeans, sweat pants* or *casual pants*, *shorts*, *T-shirts*, *sweat shirts*, and *windbreakers*.

You'll probably want to own two pairs of jeans or casual pants, one or two pairs of shorts, four or five T-shirts, one or two sweat shirts, and one windbreaker.

- *Designer jeans* can be found at flea markets—but even there they are far more expensive than regular jeans. Be aware that what you're buying is the designer's exclusive label, and that luxury can severely cut down on the number of pairs you can afford.

    Instead of picking up three pairs of jeans you might have to settle for one pair of designer jeans. If it's worth it to you—go right ahead!

- *Casual pants* can cost less than jeans, though they are not usually as sturdy as denim. Sweat pants can be even more economical. You can usually buy them in sets with sweat shirts—and, almost always, you can wear the sweat pants with other tops as well. Those can be a terrific fashion bargain because they're made of a sturdy fabric and last a long, long time.

- *Shorts* are even less expensive—because they use so much less material. You can often find running shorts in cotton or nylon with logos on the bottom, and they wear beautifully. Other types of shorts might cost more, depending on the material they're made of and how complicated their design is.

- *T-shirts* are a great fashion bargain, since they're usually made of thin cotton in very simple designs. Be aware that T-shirts and sweat shirts made of special fabrics such as nylon or silk, or purchased at special events such as rock concerts will be up to five times as expensive—you're paying for the special event logo, not the T-shirt. Tank tops are also very reasonable: You can buy them in many different colors for about the same price as T-shirts.

FASHION "EXTRAS"

These are the items you need for accessorizing your basic wardrobe. They include *shoes, sunglasses, bathing suit, beach robe, jewelry* and other accessories.

- ✪ The most expensive—and most necessary—items are shoes. You'll need your sturdy flats for school, running shoes or other special sports shoes for after school, sandals for summer and one pair of dressy shoes. The least expensive will be the sandals, especially if you choose simple rubber thongs. If you want a more elaborate sandal in leather or plastic, the cost can go up. School shoes, depending on style and material, will cost more, but you'll wear them all year and use them more than any other single item in your wardrobe. They're well worth the investment!
Special aerobics, tennis or running shoes that are made by sports manufacturing experts will cost more than basic sneakers, but their cut and fabric will be excellent. We think they're worth the investment, especially if you use them for working out or playing sports. Dress shoes, in expensive fabrics like patent leather or satin, with high

heels, can also be expensive, but it's nice to have one pair for very special occasions.

- Sunglasses are a relatively inexpensive item, unless you decide you *must* have designer shades! If you can live without the designer name, you won't break the bank paying for a good sturdy pair of sunglasses. Whatever brand you buy, be sure your shades will block out ultraviolet (UV) light to protect those beautiful eyes!
- Most girls, unless they are school swim stars, require only one bathing suit. You'll want something you can wear again and again, in sturdy fabric and good non-fading colors. Bikinis and one-piece suits cost about the same, and usually last for at least two summers. A cover-up or a short terry cloth robe is a nice extra beachwear item if it fits in your budget. If not, a sweat shirt works just as well as a cover-up!
- You'll always need extra pantyhose, knee-highs and regular socks, so be sure to set aside funds to buy them. Pantyhose and knee-highs are items that you'll probably want to buy cheaply, since pantyhose are an easy-to-rip item. You'll also want several pairs of good socks to wear under jeans or pants. Shop for these items and for your underwear—bras and panties—at discount stores to get the best bargains.
- Jewelry is an important item to almost all young women. You will have to decide which types of jewelry are most important to you—seldom can a girl's budget stretch to fit *every* type of jewelry available! If you adore necklaces but seldom wear rings, make sure to leave rings out of your budget

plans. Decide which items you like and stock up on them! Since jewelry is available in so many different styles and materials, it's best to price it yourself.

You have to make the same kind of decision about other accessories. Would you rather have two belts—or a special hat? Can you be happy without *ever* wearing hair combs? Would you die if you had to give up scarves?

You can't have it all—so decide what you really want! You might be able to get by with one belt—but want to stock up on different types of handbags. Or want a dozen scarves—but be happily indifferent to colored pantyhose!

The key is picking the most important accessories for *your* wardrobe—and buying them carefully. Like jewelry, accessories vary in price, depending on manufacturer, style and fabric. Do your own research about accessory prices—then figure out how much you can spend on the items you really want!

"DRESSY" CLOTHES

This section of your wardrobe will be the smallest, but may be the most fun to plan! This season, will you buy one or two really special mid-length dresses or one knockout floor-length outfit—or that fabulous silk pants suit you'll wear for only the best occasions?

These are the most expensive clothes you can buy—and if you're hunting for designer labels, you may be way out of your element here. Because so many of these clothes are made of very delicate fabrics, the prices will be high enough without adding a label!

- *Formals*—floor-length dresses intended for special occasions—can be pricey! The best way to economize on such purchases is to pick a dress in a sheer synthetic fabric. You can choose some wild styles but keep the cost down because you aren't buying silk or velvet—it's the best price-shopping you can do!
- *Mid-calf-length dresses*—which you can wear to weddings, big parties and semiformal dances—can cost just as much as formals, depending on manufacturer and fabric. You may want to invest more money in a mid-length dress because you'll be able to wear it to more functions than your formal. In the dressy line, mid-length dresses are usually very adaptable—and you can use your special accessories to dress it up or dress it down!
- *Dressy accessories* aren't cheap, either. You may need one special handbag for more formal occasions, but take comfort in the fact that you'll use it for years! Obviously you'll want to wear your best jewelry with dressy clothes—and you may even want to drape a cape or shawl over your shoulders! What could look more elegant?

As with any budget, set aside a small portion as your "mad" money. Someday you'll be shopping and you'll spot a fabulous item that you don't really need in your basic wardrobe—but you'll die if you don't have it! Keep this money for just such a purchase, and see how well you can blend that special item into the sensible wardrobe you've already assembled!

It may take some figuring—and re-figuring—but you'll find that you can pull together a super wardrobe that fits into your budget and dazzles your friends!

Making It All Work

By now, you've learned all the fundamental rules of fashion wisdom. You know your own basic type and look. You're a whiz at matching clothes colors to your own unique coloring, and you know how to jump effortlessly from one mood to another. You're the accessory wizard on your block—nobody can stretch a wardrobe the way you can!—and you're experimenting all the time with recycling tricks to give you even *more* great looks! You know which of your features to play up—and how to camouflage your "problem areas." You've leaped the hurdle of shopping—alone or in a group—and you're increasingly conscious of your budget.

Now it's time to put it all together! Let your fashion guides show you how they stuck to their budgets while choosing the "perfect" purchases for them:

☆☆☆

MARCY'S WARDROBE

Our athletic blonde, *Marcy*, needs a little of everything, so she has to budget carefully. How does she manage it?

- 2 pairs jeans: One light blue faded denim, the other traditional dark blue denim
- 1 knee-length camel-colored wool skirt
- 2 blouses: A long-sleeved ivory cotton blend and a short-sleeved soft yellow and ivory horizontal-striped cotton
- 3 sweaters: A mint green wool V-neck, an ivory synthetic-blend turtleneck and a lilac cotton-blend crew neck
- 1 pair thin powder-blue seersucker pants
- 2 school dresses: A pink and lilac print dress and a black/yellow horizontal stripe
- 1 mint green cotton-blend sweat suit with hooded collar

- ⊙ 1 blue nylon/cotton windbreaker
- ⊙ 3 T-shirts: One pink, one mint green print, and one black with large lilac polka dots
- ⊙ 1 stenciled soft yellow sweat shirt
- ⊙ 1 pair brown penny loafers (for school)
- ⊙ 1 pair white aerobics shoes with pink laces
- ⊙ 3 pairs thick white socks
- ⊙ 3 pairs beige pantyhose
- ⊙ 2 pairs earrings: pink and black squares; round lilac and blue stripes
- ⊙ 1 tan leather belt with a gold buckle

Marcy is now equipped for every major occasion on her calendar—and in colors and fabrics that suit her wonderfully!

Since Marcy spends most of her time in casual settings and almost never attends formal parties, she elects to leave dressy clothes out of her shopping list on this trip. She'd prefer to put any extra money toward some mad and marvelous purchase that she just might spot as she walks through the department store aisles!

☆☆☆

LINDA'S WARDROBE

Linda, our petite brunette, leans toward dressy styles, since she's a romantic type. She'd rather *look* terrific than be able to move with an athlete's freedom—so her fashion choices will feature fewer casual clothes. And her dark, vivid coloring will look best with bold, bright colors like deep red, royal purple and emerald green. Because she's proud of her pretty eyes and developing curves, Linda will seek clothes that play up these features.

Here's how Linda puts together a dazzling wardrobe that stays within her budget:

- 1 cherry red corduroy jumpsuit
- 2 snug-fitting sweaters: A short-sleeved V-neck emerald cotton blend and a long-sleeved V-neck deep purple wool
- 2 mid-calf-length skirts: An A-line cotton blend in white and gray vertical stripes, and an A-line beige wool
- 1 white linen long-sleeved blouse
- 1 pair gray-beige tweed pants with a belt
- 1 navy blue shirtdress with a belt
- 1 pair dark denim jeans
- 1 yellow sweat shirt with logo
- 2 tank tops: A white with an intricate abstract design, and a purple tank with lace trim
- 1 pair sunglasses
- 1 pair flat-heeled gray skimmers
- 1 pair high-heeled black satin pumps for dress clothes
- 6 pairs pantyhose
- 2 pairs earrings: One pair of gold love knots and a pair of imitation amethyst studs
- 1 floor-length purple and black formal dress

Linda prefers to spend the bulk of her time in social, often dress-up pursuits and she considers a full-length formal essential. Therefore, it's easy for her to make the decision to skip a bathing suit and beach robe on this shopping trip. When she saves money from her after-school job, she can look for summerwear.

☆☆☆

KIM'S WARDROBE

Kim, our dazzling redhead, has tastes that run toward the contemporary, rock 'n' roll look, and she looks best in colors that complement her fabulous red hair—like forest green, tawny brown, black and pale red. Kim's idea of "fashion heaven" is a big investment in accessories! She prefers to dress up simple clothes with rock 'n' roll accessories to show off her personality—so let's see how Kim spends *her* fashion dollars:

- ✪ 1 pair tight black jeans
- ✪ 1 ivory and black vertical-striped rayon blouse
- ✪ 1 forest green long-sleeved cotton blouse
- ✪ 2 skirts: A black denim and a tawny brown corduroy
- ✪ 2 long-sleeved sweaters: A pale red cotton blend with red sequins and a lavender V-neck

- 1 pair brown leather pants
- 2 scoop-necked leotards in soft blue and misty yellow
- 1 black linen vest
- 2 pairs light blue jeans
- 1 long-sleeved gray sweat shirt with silver studs
- 1 pair ivory running shorts
- 3 T-shirts: Misty yellow, soft blue, and red with a black logo
- 1 silver belt
- 1 tropical print bikini in forest green, tawny brown and pale red
- 1 pair soft ivory kid boots
- 3 pairs sparkly knee-high socks
- 1 silver necklace set with ruby stones
- 1 set multicolored, 6-tier bracelets
- 3 pairs black sparkly pantyhose
- 2 pairs dangling earrings: One pair of turquoise hearts rimmed in black, the other pair deep green squares

Kim's "splurge" item is her new pair of leather pants. Yet her list balances the needs of school and casual wear with her identity as a rock 'n' roll type. No important item for her contemporary lifestyle has been excluded.

Marcy, Linda and Kim now know *who they are*, fashion-wise—and so do you! You now have the tools to put together a great wardrobe—and one that won't kill your budget! Remember, all it takes is patience, imagination and common sense. Your own particular style may deepen or change as you grow older, but remember that no matter what your age, *fashion can always be fun*!

SMART TALK Has It All!

Some of the best tips for fashion, fun and friendship are in the Smart Talk series. Learn how to look and feel your greatest, create your own personal style, and show the world the great new you! Smart Talk points the way:

Skin Deep
Looking Good
Eating Pretty
Feeling Fit
Finishing Touches—Manners with Style
Now You're Talking—Winning with Words
Dream Rooms—Decorating with Flair
Great Parties—How to Plan Them
How to Make (and Keep) Friends